D1072755

CAMBRIDGE TEXTS IN THE
HISTORY OF POLITICAL THOUGHT

——

SIR JOHN FORTESCUE
On the Laws and Governance of England

CAMBRIDGE TEXTS IN THE HISTORY OF POLITICAL THOUGHT

Series editors

RAYMOND GEUSS
Lecturer in Social and Political Sciences, University of Cambridge

QUENTIN SKINNER
Regius Professor of Modern History in the University of Cambridge

Cambridge Texts in the History of Political Thought is now firmly established as the major student textbook series in political theory. It aims to make available to students all the most important texts in the history of western political thought, from ancient Greece to the early twentieth century. All the familiar classic texts will be included but the series does at the same time seek to enlarge the conventional canon by incorporating an extensive range of less well-known works, many of them never before available in a modern English edition. Wherever possible, texts are published in complete and unabridged form, and translations are specially commissioned for the series. Each volume contains a critical introduction together with chronologies, biographical sketches, a guide to further reading and any necessary glossaries and textual apparatus. When completed, the series will aim to offer an outline of the entire evolution of western political thought.

For a list of titles published in the series, please see end of book.

SIR JOHN FORTESCUE

On the Laws and Governance of England

EDITED BY

SHELLEY LOCKWOOD

Board of Continuing Education,
University of Cambridge

CAMBRIDGE
UNIVERSITY PRESS

Published by the Press Syndicate of the University of Cambridge
The Pitt Building, Trumpington Street, Cambridge CB2 1RP
40 West 20th Street, New York, NY 10011–4211, USA
10 Stamford Road, Oakleigh, Melbourne 3166, Australia

© in the edition, introduction and editorial matter
Cambridge University Press 1997

First published 1997

Printed in Great Britain at the University Press, Cambridge

A catalogue record for this book is available from the British Library

Library of Congress cataloguing in publication data

Fortescue, John, Sir, 1394?–1476?
[De laudibus legum Angliae. English]
Sir John Fortescue: on the laws and governance of England /
edited by Shelley Lockwood.
p.   cm. – (Cambridge texts in the history of political thought)
Contains *In praise of the laws of England* and *The governance of England*.
ISBN 0 521 43445 9 (hardback)
1. Law – England.   2. England – Politics and government.
I. Lockwood, Shelley.   II. Fortescue, John, Sir, 1394?–1476?
Difference between an absolute and limited monarchy.   III. Title.
IV. Series.
KD600.F6713   1997
349.42–dc20   [344.2] 96–14038   CIP

ISBN 0 521 43445 9 hardback
ISBN 0 521 58996 7 paperback

For my parents with love

Contents

Acknowledgements

My former students have been foremost in my mind during the final preparation of this volume and I thank them for their interest and enthusiasm for the study of political thought and for helping me to remember that things are rarely self-explanatory. My greatest debt of thanks, and one which I am delighted to acknowledge here, is to Quentin Skinner who, as lecturer, research supervisor, colleague and friend, has been a constant source of inspiration and encouragement. Brendan Bradshaw, who first introduced me to the thought of Sir John Fortescue, and Jimmy Burns, whose work stimulated my initial research, have also helped and advised at crucial stages and I hope that they will enjoy seeing Fortescue back in print and being read and discussed. Many other scholarly friends have also contributed a great deal to my understanding of the work of Sir John Fortescue through their expertise and willingness to enter into debate, especially Annabel Brett, George Garnett, Magnus Ryan and, above all, John Watts.

I should also like to thank the Master and Fellows of Christ's College, Cambridge under whose auspices (as A. H. Lloyd Research Fellow) I conducted much of the research which informs my Introduction in this volume. I thank the staff of the Rare Books Room at the University Library in Cambridge for their cheerful forbearance. Several people from the Press have been involved in the production of this volume, but I should especially like to thank Elaine Corke, whose commitment to clarity and patient good humour has eased the final stages considerably, and also the Series Editors for their helpful comments at an earlier stage.

Finally, the love and support of Richard Bailey and of my family is of infinite value to me in everything I do and I thank them for it with all my heart.

Editor's note on the texts

The text of *In Praise of the Laws of England* is largely the version (see Note on the translations) edited by Chrimes (Cambridge, 1942). Chrimes' text is a collation of the three extant manuscripts (Cambridge University Library, Ff.5.22, British Library Harleian MSS 1757, and Bodleian Library Digby MS 198) and the text printed by Edward Whitchurche *c.*1545 (probably taken from the original or a copy of it). The original manuscript has not survived, but it may have been the version contained in the Cottonian Library MSS Otho B 1 which perished in the fire of 1731.

The work now known universally as *The Governance of England* was not so called until Plummer's edition of 1885. It was first known as 'Of the difference between an absolute and limited monarchy.' Plummer's edition is a collation of the ten extant manuscripts, but is primarily based on Bodleian Library Laud MS 593. The present text is a translation (see Note on the translations) of Plummer's edition.

The notes to both these texts owe a great deal to the previous editors, although it has not been possible to reproduce the volume of material contained in their editions. Instead, I have given revised and up-dated textual and bibliographical references so that the reader can see the range of sources used by Fortescue and is able to find further information as required. All quotations from medieval English sources have been modernised.

Note on the translations

In Praise of the Laws of England is an amended version of Chrimes' translation (Cambridge, 1942). I have retained his familiar and elegant words and phrases as far as possible, but some alterations have been made. Where these involve a significant change in meaning, the reader's attention is drawn to this in the notes. I have also removed the archaic 'th' endings; for example, 'Perfect love casteth out fear' becomes 'Perfect love casts out fear.' A major difference not referred to in the notes is the translation of the key terms 'politicum et regale' and 'tantum regale'; I have followed Fortescue's own translation of these terms as 'political and royal' and 'only royal'. 'Dominium' is always translated as 'dominion' and 'regimen' as 'government'. Fortescue uses several verbs meaning 'to rule' – 'regere', 'regulare', 'dominare', 'imperare', 'principare', 'praesse', 'gubernare' – and Chrimes did not differentiate between them. I have translated 'gubernare' as 'govern' and 'regulare' as 'regulate', but the others are left as 'rule'.

The Governance of England is a modernised version of the text edited by Plummer (Oxford, 1885). Given the difficulty of the language for the non-expert, this has meant a translation into modern English. I have, however, tried to be as literal as possible and not to resort to paraphrase. Bridging the gap between the way we spoke and thought in the fifteenth century and the way we speak and think now can be highly misleading. To illustrate the nature of my translation, here are a couple of sentences from chapter 19, first Plummer's transcription and then my translation:

Ffor all such thynges come off impotencie, as doyth power to be syke or wex olde. And trewly, yff þe kyng do thus, he shall do þerby dayly more almes, þan shall be do be all the ffundacions þat euer were made in Englond. Ffor euery man off þe lande shal by this ffundacion euery day þe the meryer, þe surer, ffare þe better in is body and all his godis, as euery wyse man mey well conseyue.

For all such things come of impotency, as does power to be sick or to grow old. And truly, if the king does thus, he shall do thereby daily more alms than shall be done by all the foundations that were ever made in England. For every man of the land shall by this foundation be the merrier, the surer and fare the better in his body and all his goods, as every wise man may well conceive.

All Latin phrases in the original have been translated into English and put inside inverted commas. A particular problem was the translation of 'counsel' and its variants; given the fact that Fortescue is almost always referring to the institution, I have translated this as 'council'.

Introduction

Throughout this introduction, references to primary sources are
given in the form of author, title and section of work, page number;
e.g. (Aquinas, *On Princely Government*, II.i, 7); the page reference
is to the edition listed in the **Select bibliography, primary
sources**. The exception to this is Fortescue, where the page reference is to this volume unless otherwise stated. Secondary works
are given in footnotes with a full reference of author, title and
publication details, unless they appear in the **Select bibliography**,
in which case they are given in the form of author and short version of the title.

Sir John Fortescue (*c.*1395 – *c.*1477) was undoubtedly the major
English political theorist of the fifteenth century. His works are
famous, above all, for their vision of the English polity as a
'dominion political and royal', ruled by common law, and they have
been widely quoted and used over the past five hundred years. This
very popularity, however, has resulted in their original meaning
falling victim to the various purposes of his commentators.

The process of distortion began in the sixteenth century, when
the development and strengthening of both the monarchy and the
institution of parliament led to a division and potential conflict of
power between the two. In attempting to deal with this problem,
political writers of the late sixteenth and seventeenth centuries
interpreted Fortescue's 'political and royal dominion' in support
of their own projects to define the respective spheres of king and
parliament. Thus for over three hundred years, Fortescue was cited

primarily as an authority on the nature of the English 'constitution'. Since the end of the nineteenth century, however, his work has been more frequently used as an historical source; he has been taken as a simple mirror, a straightforward recorder and commentator on events and institutions as they actually were, rather than as a reflective and critical political theorist. As a more detailed picture of the workings of fifteenth-century law and government has been produced by legal and political historians, Fortescue's account has been dismissed as simply 'wrong', not to mention 'smug', 'naive', 'crude', and 'distorted by the romanticism of the ageing and exiled patriot'.

As a result, the recovery of Fortescue's original intentions has become a task akin to archaeological excavation, carefully removing the accumulated layers of interpretation. Nevertheless the task is more than worthwhile, both for historians of political thought and for historians of fifteenth-century English law and government, for we cannot recover Fortescue's original meaning without first gaining some knowledge of the man, of the resources available to him and of the historical context in and for which he wrote. We shall then see him as writing in response to a real crisis of governance in the mid-fifteenth century – not merely reflecting, but reflecting on the workings of contemporary law and governance.

Following the triumphant kingship of Henry V (1413–1422), the war, debt and disorder which marked the reign of the incapacitated Henry VI created a widely perceived crisis of governance in England from the 1440s to the 1470s. By 1450, the Crown had huge debts, Normandy was lost and there had been massive abuses of the king's patronage (most notably by William de la Pole, duke of Suffolk). There were factional rifts in the council, overspending in the king's household made a mockery of the notion that the king should 'live of his own' and in the localities there was violence and corruption in the administration of justice. The cluster of abuses – retaining, livery, maintenance, embracery, riot and forcible entry – which have, since Plummer's edition of *The Governance*, been referred to under the heading 'bastard feudalism' (Plummer edn, 1885, 15–16), were perceived to be on the increase despite statutory legislation against them. It is hard to quantify these abuses, let alone to judge their actual effect on the working of local government,[1] but they feature heavily in the political literature of the period, especially in poems and ballads.[2] Frustrations at these injustices were summed up in the 'Complaint' of Jack Cade (1450) which paints a vivid picture of an impoverished king who 'can not pay for his meat nor drink and owes more than ever any king of England ever owed', and who is surrounded by 'insatiable, covetous, malicious,' persons who 'daily inform him that good is evil and evil is good'.[3]

Although blame was mainly laid at the feet of 'evil ministers', the weakness of the king himself was an inescapable and crucial fact of political life. Henry VI succeeded his father in 1422 at the age of nine months. He took up the reins of government in 1437, but suffered bouts of mental breakdown from 1453 onwards.[4] This absence of the single unifying and controlling will at the centre of government represented a failure of the king in the key duties of his public office – peace and justice – and a negation of the virtues expected of a monarch.[5] A chronically weak king was as much of a threat as a tyrant because he would lack that constant and perpetual will to justice which was the sworn duty of his office.

Fortescue's works, in response to this crisis, form a coherent and extended argument for justice against tyranny, for public against private interest. The precedence of private over public good is seen to be the definition of tyranny because it leads to injustice and oppression: 'covetise' (desiring and having more than one's own) in one or some produces a corresponding poverty (having less than one's own) in others, and the peace and tranquillity of the realm is thereby shattered. Justice (each having one's own) is to be ensured by means of natural and human laws which are also sacred because they are divine in origin. Fortescue's works are thus dominated by a concern for justice which is seen to be the touchstone for the legitimacy and proper functioning of political authority. His per-

---

[1] Bellamy, *Criminal Law and Society*; Bellamy, *Bastard Feudalism and the Law*; Powell, *Kingship, Law and Society*.
[2] Kail, *Political and Other Poems*; Scattergood, *Politics and Poetry*.
[3] Harvey, *Jack Cade's Rebellion*, p.189.
[4] Griffiths, *The Reign of Henry VI*; Watts, *Henry VI and the Politics of Kingship*; Wolffe, *Henry VI*.
[5] Watts, *Henry VI and the Politics of Kingship*.

spective is that of someone who thinks politically about law; he was a self-consciously analytical and highly experienced lawyer and government official.

John Fortescue was one of a growing group of lay professionals.[6] He attended Lincoln's Inn, of which he was Governor four times before 1430. Between 1421 and 1436 he was elected eight times to parliament. He was created serjeant-at-law in July 1438, by 1441 was a king's serjeant and became Chief Justice of the King's Bench in January 1442, after which he was knighted. He served as justice of the peace thirty-five times in seventeen counties and boroughs, received over seventy commissions of *oyer et terminer*, assize, etc., attended meetings of the council and tried petitions for parliament.

He was present at the battle of Towton (1461), following which he was attainted, having fled to Edinburgh with Henry VI and Queen Margaret. Whilst in Scotland he wrote a series of pro-Lancastrian succession tracts, including *On the Nature of the Law of Nature* (Clermont edn, 1869).[7] In July 1463, he went across the Channel with the court to St Mihiel in Bar where, by his own account, they lived in poverty (Clermont edn, 1869, 23–5). He remained in exile in France for seven years, travelling occasionally to Paris. During this time, he wrote *In Praise of the Laws of England*, possibly translated the works of Alain Chartier,[8] and wrote a 'memorandum to Louis XI' urging an invasion to restore Henry and establish peace between England and France (Clermont edn, 1869, 34–5). On the 4th of April 1471 he landed at Weymouth with Queen Margaret and Prince Edward. On the 5th of May, at the battle of Tewkesbury, Prince Edward was killed and Fortescue was captured. Thereafter he wrote his *Declaration upon certain writings sent out of Scotland* in which he repudiated his earlier, pro-Lancastrian succession tracts (Clermont edn, 1869, 523–41). He was subsequently pardoned (*Rot. Parl.* VI, 69 and Clermont edn, 1869,

---

[6] Clough, *Profession, Vocation and Culture*; Genet, 'Ecclesiastics and Political Theory', in R.B. Dobson (ed.), *The Church, Patronage and Politics*.

[7] Gill, *Politics and Propaganda in Fifteenth-Century England*; Litzen, *A War of Roses and Lilies*.

[8] Blayney, 'Sir John Fortescue and Alain Chartier's "Traite de l'Esperance"'; Blayney (ed.), *Fifteenth Century Translations of Alain Chartier*; and Blayney (ed.), *A Familiar Dialogue*.

43) and became a member of Edward IV's council. We do not know when *The Governance* was first drafted, but it is clear that an updated and revised version was presented to Edward IV after 1471.

Fortescue's credentials as an authority on the formal workings of law and government in fifteenth-century England are thus unimpeachable; not only had he been directly engaged in the central and local administration of justice and sat in both council and parliament, but he had also had a period of political exile which gave him the time and perspective to reflect and write in some detail about the law and governance of his country. But in addition to his practical experience and expertise, Fortescue also used the resources of contemporary theory as a basis on which to construct his work.

The political thought of late medieval England was dominated by the moralising tradition of mirror-for-princes literature,[9] concentrating on the duties of kingship and the virtues of the king. The philosophical framework was scholastic, in particular the Thomist interpretation of Aristotle. The key term was 'governance', the 'gubernator' or governor being the helmsman who directs the ship safely to port – 'to govern is to guide that which is governed to its appointed end' (Aquinas, *On Princely Government*, I.xiv, 73). The 'end' to which the governed were directed was the Aristotelian secondary happiness of living in society in accordance with the moral virtues (Aristotle, *Nicomachean Ethics*, x, 331), which, according to the Thomist gloss, would ultimately be rewarded by *beatitudo* or eternal salvation. In broad terms, the means to those ends were the king, law and the grace of God; in specific terms, the means were to be determined through counsel and deliberation, that is, by the light of reason – 'man has reason, by the light of which his actions are directed to their end' (Aquinas, *On Princely Government*, I.i, 3). This was the substance of the practical science of politics.

Among the most popular ways in which philosophical knowledge was transmitted were the *florilegia* or anthologies, such as the *Auctoritates Aristotelis* (Hamesse edn, 1974) which Fortescue used. The fifteenth century saw an increased use of the vernacular in England, a prime example of which are the works of Bishop Reginald Pecock

---

[9] Genet (ed.), *Four English Political Tracts*; Green, *Poets and Prince Pleasers*; Guenée, *States and Rulers*, pp. 37–44.

(*c*.1395–*c*.1460), written in English for a lay audience,[10] and there were very many translations into English from French, Latin and Italian.[11] Fortescue's sources include Poggio Bracciolini's translation (into Latin from Greek) of Diodorus Siculus' *Ancient Histories* and the *Isagogue of Moral Philosophy* of Leonardo Bruni. Fortescue himself may have translated the works of Alain Chartier (Chartier, *A Familiar Dialogue*)[12] and comparisons have recently been made between Fortescue and the work of Jean de Terre Vermeille.[13]

There were many general historical sources, such as the Old Testament, Geoffrey of Monmouth's *History of the Kings of Britain*, Higden's *Polychronicon* and numerous chronicles and genealogies,[14] as well as the works of chivalry known as books of 'urbanity' or courtesy books which usually contained a mixture of heraldry and a version of Vegetius' *De Rei Militarii*, as, for example, Sir John Paston's 'Grete Boke'. In addition to these, there were also English institutional works, such as the *Dialogue of the Exchequer* and the *Modus Tenendi Parlamentum,* and the literature and sources of the common law.[15] Of the lawyers, Bracton's work was perhaps the most used, providing as it did a framework for the discussion of English law; a framework gathered largely from Roman civil law, via the work of the glossator Azo.[16] Bracton was particularly useful to discussions of kingship and law because of his synthesis between the Roman law *princeps* and the English *rex*; he stresses that kingship is an office and gives *lex* and those learned in the law a very high status (Bracton, *On the Laws and Customs of England*, I, 305).

The history of the development of English government adds a further dimension to these theories: in the thirteenth and fourteenth centuries, the concept of the *communitas regni* developed greatly, as evidenced by the addition of a fourth clause to the coronation oath, binding the king to keep the laws which he and the people 'will have

[10] Doe, 'Fifteenth-Century Concepts of Law'; Patrough, *Reginald Pecock*.
[11] Genet, 'Ecclesiastics and Political Theory' in Dobson (ed.), *The Church, Patronage and Politics in the Fifteenth Century*; Mitchell, *John Tiptoft*; Weiss, *Humanism in England*.
[12] Blayney, 'Sir John Fortescue and Alain Chartier's "Traité de l'Espérance"'
[13] Burns, *Lordship, Kingship and Empire*, ch. 3.
[14] Kingsford, *English Historical Literature*.
[15] Plucknett, *Early English Legal Literature*; Genet, 'Droit et Histoire'.
[16] Maitland, *Selected Passages from the Work of Bracton and Azo*; Seipp, 'Roman Legal Categories in Early Common Law' in T.G. Watkin (ed.), *Legal Record and Historical Reality*, pp. 9–36.

chosen',[17] and with the growth of parliament as the representative institution of the realm.[18] References to the oath and to parliament are recurrent features of the political polemic of the fifteenth century.

A further strand of vocabulary and associated theory comes from ancient Rome by way of the work of St Augustine. Augustine cited Scipio's definition (from Cicero's *De Re Publica*) of *res publica* as *res populi* (the property of the people), where 'a people' is a 'numerous gathering united in fellowship by a common sense of right and a community of interest' (*City of God* XIX.xxi; *De Re Publica* I.xxv). The language of *res publica* was still relatively new in fifteenth-century England, and the author of the *Boke of Noblesse* (*c.*1449) attempted to define and translate the terms: *res publica* becomes 'common profit' and the definition combines Ciceronian (Augustine) and Aristotelian (Aquinas) vocabulary. The author of *Somnium Vigilantis* (1459), a work at one time attributed to Fortescue, also used this language extensively.

These various strands led to a general theory of polity-centred kingship: an hereditary monarch who ruled by his will, but after due consultation with, and in the interests of, his subjects, and who was bound to keep the laws of his realm and to ask the consent of his people for taxation. Although there existed no means for coercing the king, there was nevertheless a strong sense of obligation to a common sphere in which king and people shared; a public sphere, the mode of designation for which was the abstract notion of 'the Crown': 'in the figure of the Crown, the rule and polity of the realm are presented' (a parliamentary sermon of 1436). Bracton's concept of the Crown had included both the communal sense and the important further notion of inalienability:

> a thing quasi-sacred is a thing fiscal (*res fiscalis*), which cannot be given away or be sold or transferred upon another person by the prince or ruling king (*rex regnante*), and those things make the Crown what it is, and they regard to common utility such as peace and justice.
>
> (Bracton, *On the Laws and Customs of England*, II, 58)

[17] Schramm, *A History of the English Coronation*, pp. 75–9.
[18] Edwards, 'The *Plena Potestas* of English Parliamentary Representatives' in F.W. Powicke (ed.) *Oxford Essays Presented to H.E. Salter*; Pronay and Taylor, *Modus Tenendi Parlamentum*; Roskell, *Parliament and Politics*, I. 1–4.

Just as kingship was a public office, so the kingdom was public property and must not be alienated. A corollary of the idea of non-alienation was that the body politic or realm had the status of a person under age (a minor) in need of a guardian or tutor. Thus the king became guardian of the realm and the realm consequently had the privileges of a minor with regard to its property. In that way the public sphere was protected.[19]

The realm was thus perceived to be a single organism with an appointed end towards which it had a natural desire and inclination; that organism was a body politic with one man as head, whose will unified and ruled the body as a whole, and the end towards which it tended was the common weal of peace and justice. The realm was corporately visible when the king was in his parliament and it was represented by the abstract notion of the Crown. The king was guardian of the Crown; he could not alienate its property, nor could he take his subjects' goods without their consent. The king had to ensure that justice was done through the laws and had himself to be the 'living law' when equity required. The king took an oath to that effect at his coronation when he was 'elected' by the people and anointed with holy oil.[20] But the king was also minister of God and of a higher estate than ordinary men, as evidenced by his sacral powers[21] (Fortescue, *De Titulo Edwardi*, ch.X, in Clermont edn (1869), p.85*). He was undoubtedly the key to good governance, the man at the helm. So, to what use did Sir John Fortescue CJKB put these ideas, how did he adapt them to suit his needs, what response did he make to the circumstances in which he wrote?

Fortescue clearly created his central concept of 'dominium politicum et regale' from a combination of the sources mentioned in the preceding section and his own experience of law and government in England. The concept is developed throughout Fortescue's works and a progression can be traced from the philosophical origins of the first book of *On the Nature of the Law of Nature*, through the reforming ideal of *In Praise of the Laws of England* to the concrete, institutional reforms of *The Governance*.

[19] Kantorowicz, *The King's Two Bodies*; Schramm, *A History of the English Coronation*.
[20] Ullman, 'Thomas Becket's Miraculous Oil', *Journal of Theological Studies*, (n.s. VIII, 1957), 129–33; McKenna, 'The Coronation Oil of the Yorkist Kings'.
[21] Bloch, *The Royal Touch*.

Book I of *On the Nature of the Law of Nature* contains a great deal of the scholastic theory referred to above: Fortescue's main sources are the Bible, Augustine, Aristotle and Aquinas. It provides a substantial theoretical context within which to examine *In Praise of the Laws of England* and *The Governance* since Fortescue's understanding of the fundamental concepts of law, justice, and kingship are first revealed in this work.[22] Using Aristotle by way of Aquinas, Fortescue states that kingship originated under the law of nature (Appendix A); it was established by natural law which is divine, and its purpose is to guide people to a virtuous life (*Nature*, in Clermont edn (1869), I.xliv, 243). This in turn will be rewarded with eternal salvation, through the grace of God, 'for it is not by law only, but rather by grace that we attain unto beatitude' (*Nature*, in Clermont edn (1869), II, xxxiv, 292). *On the Nature of the Law of Nature* Book I establishes that the office of the king is to rule rightly and that he must rule by means of the law which is the sacred bond of human society (*Nature*, in Clermont edn (1869), I.xviii and xxx). It is also in this work that we have Fortescue's most detailed account of 'dominium politicum et regale'.

Here he states that the government of the realm is 'political' because it 'is ruled by the administration of many (*est plurium dispensatione regulatum*)', and 'royal' because the subjects cannot make laws without 'the authority of the king (*regia auctoritate*)' and because 'the realm . . . is possessed by kings and their heirs successively in hereditary right' (Appendix A). It is also made clear that the 'political' element does not constitute an infringement of the king's power or liberty, because the ability to do wrong is not power, but lack of power or impotence (Appendix A). A further important point is made in *On the Nature of the Law of Nature*: that the king who rules politically must also be able to rule 'only royally (*tantum regale*)' when necessary either for reasons of equity (*Nature*, Clermont edn (1869), I.xxiv) or in time of rebellion (*Nature*, Clermont edn (1869), I.xxv).

---

[22] Because of the importance of the theory established in *On the Nature of the Law of Nature*, three relevant extracts have been included in this volume (Appendix A). It should be remembered, however, that the work forms part of Fortescue's writings on succession and addresses fundamentally different issues from those contained in the works edited in this volume. For a discussion of the work, see Litzen, *A War of Roses and Lilies*.

Turning now to the argument of the two texts contained in this volume: *In Praise of the Laws of England* is a dialogue in Latin between Prince Edward (son of Henry VI and Queen Margaret) and the Chancellor. It is a didactic dialogue of the master-student variety, as, for example, the *Dialogue of the Exchequer* and later, Christopher St German's *Doctor and Student*. It is formally structured: the Chancellor 'moves' that the Prince should study the laws, the Prince gives a 'replication' to the Chancellor's motion, in response, the Chancellor strengthens his motion and 'proves' his case, he then summarises (*epilogat*) the 'effect of his argument' (chs.I-VI). Thereafter, the Chancellor 'shows' or 'teaches', whilst the Prince 'questions' and 'interpellates'. This part of the dialogue is Aristotelian in character, much like one of Fortescue's sources, Leonardo Bruni's *Isagogue of Moral Philosophy*.

Seeing the Prince spending all his time on military training, the Chancellor seeks to teach him that the prime duty of the office of kingship is justice, which is to be achieved by means of the law. Having proved the value of law, using a combination of arguments and examples taken from Deuteronomy, Aristotle, Roman law and Bruni (*Praise*, chs.I-VI, pp. 4–13), the Chancellor goes on to show the Prince that the English 'political and royal' kingship which operates by means of 'political and royal' law is preferable to the 'only royal' kingship of the French civil law system because it provides a better defence against tyranny and is a better guarantor of justice (*Praise*, chs.IX, XII-XIV pp. 17–24). He also demonstrates to the Prince that the laws of England are the best because they are uniquely suited to the realm of England (*Praise*, XV and XXIX, pp. 25, 43).

In Praise of the Laws of England is thus a rhetorical work: the author seeks to persuade the reader of the value of English law and government *as it should be* and suggests ways in which reform might be undertaken. Fortescue's concern was to establish a defence of political monarchy on the grounds of reason, law and justice and thereby to provide a theory to fit the practice of that monarchy *as it should be*. In his account of 'dominium politicum et regale' Fortescue was not fitting practice to existing theory since, despite his claim to have taken his argument from Aquinas (*Praise*, ch.IX, p. 18; *Governance*, ch. 1, p. 84), his synthesis appears original, nor was he creating a theory to which practice in reality conformed, which it did not. He was creating a theory to which he felt English practice *should ideally* conform: England should conform to 'dominium politicum et regale' because that was the best form of *dominium* for England.

In Praise of the Laws of England is therefore to be seen as a critical and reforming work rather than as complacent or merely descriptive. Any pretence that he is describing the actual situation is dropped in the chapters on the administration of justice in the localities, a matter in which Fortescue was himself experienced – the titles of the chapters state that this is how jurors 'ought to be' chosen and informed (*Praise*, chs.XXV and XXVI, pp. 36, 38). The work should therefore be read as an account of how English law and government *should ideally* be, it is a kind of *modus gubernandi regnum*, along the lines of the early institutional manuals, the *Dialogue of the Exchequer* and the *Modus Tenendi Parlamentum* (Pronay and Taylor edn, 1980, 32). Fortescue is instilling faith in an idealised system of government, thereby highlighting the gap between ideal and actual in order to stimulate reform.

Pride and praise is most genuine (perhaps unsurprisingly) in the sections of the work concerning the English legal profession, its status and organisation (*Praise*, chs.XLVIII-LI, pp. 66–75). A picture is drawn of a unique and distinct body of substantive law, taught in a special academy – the Inns of Court. Trained lawyers are of high standing: following Roman law, but probably taken from Bracton, Fortescue states that law is 'holy (*sanctum*)' and that lawyers are 'priests (*sacerdotes*)' (*Praise*, ch.III, pp. 6–7). The serjeants-at-law are especially favoured; they are *character indelibis* and therefore survive intact the demise of the king (*Praise*, ch.L, p. 70 and notes). It is remarkable how much detail Fortescue gives on the Inns and the legal profession, given that the Chancellor states at the beginning of the work that the Prince shall not himself have to undertake such training. These sections give a solid grounding for the uniqueness of English law and for the status of law and lawyers in the body politic – they know the mysteries of the law which binds the realm together and by means of which it shall attain peace and justice.

It is in seeking to explain the nature and value of English law for England (in preference to the civil law), that the Chancellor embarks on his account of the origins of the realm of England and its form of rule. These well-known passages are the key to the meaning of Fortescue's theory of 'dominium politicum et regale' for England.

Using Aristotle and Cicero (via Augustine), Fortescue states that a people does not constitute a body unless it has a head. Therefore, he continues, when a people 'wills' to 'erect itself into a body politic (*se erigere in corpus politicum*)', it must always set up one person for the government of that body and that person is usually called 'king' (*Praise*, ch.XIII, p. 20). The analogy is then made between the people as embryo and the kingdom (*regnum*) as the developed physical body, regulated by a head or king. Most importantly, the kingdom 'issues from the people (*ex populo erumpit*)' and 'exists as a body mystical (*corpus extat mysticum*)'. And 'thus the kingdom of England blossomed forth (*prorupit*) into a political and royal dominion out of Brutus' band of Trojans' (*Praise*, ch.XIII p. 22). *Corpus mysticum* is a theological concept signifying an undying corporation, a *universitas*. It therefore represents a more sophisticated theory than that of the organological concept of the body as head and members because it allows for the perpetuation of the plurality of the realm (Kantorowicz, 1957).

Fortescue tells the same story in *The Governance*: a 'fellowship' came into England with Brutus, 'willing to be united and made a body politic called a realm, having a head to govern it'. They 'chose' Brutus to be 'their head and king'. Then 'they and he upon this incorporation, institution, and uniting of themselves into a realm, ordained the same realm to be ruled and justified by such laws as they all would assent to' (*Governance*, ch.2, p. 86; *Praise*, ch.XXXIV, p. 48).[23] This law is thus to be known as 'political and royal'; 'political' because all assent to it, and 'royal' because it is 'administered by a king'. The verb used here is 'ministrare' and this is therefore associated with the king's role as *minister Dei* and with his guardianship of the realm. The origin of the body politic or body mystical which is the realm of England is thus the will of those who came to England with Brutus; they willed to be a body politic and so they incorporated themselves, the natural corollary of which was that they chose a head to govern them. The governance of England is clearly based on consent.

[23] Schramm, *A History of the English Coronation.*

The crucial relationship is said to be that between the heart and the head (*Praise*, ch.XIII pp. 20–1). Following Aristotle, the heart is the first formed part of the embryo, the first organ or member to have life. In the body politic, the heart is 'the intention of the people (*intencio populi*)' which contains the blood or 'political provision for the interest of the people'. I have altered Chrimes' translation of two key phrases in this passage in order to bring out the meaning more clearly. For '*intencio populi*' Chrimes had 'will of the people' which would imply *voluntas*, but this is precisely what the people no longer have once they have incorporated themselves because they had to choose a king to be head and to provide the single unifying will. Also, I have altered Chrimes' 'forethought' as a translation of '*provisionem*' to the more literal 'provision', both in order to maintain the original sense of 'looking out for' and also to preserve the connection with 'providence' which in turn was associated with 'prudence';[24] 'provision', 'providence' or 'prudence' was the political virtue needed for the proper deliberation about the means to the ends of human life – 'from prudence come choice and deliberation and all actions depend on them' (Bruni, *Isagogue*, 281).

The implications of these ideas for the nature of the governance of England and the constitution of the body politic become clearer if we look at the work of Aquinas, perhaps Fortescue's major source. For Aquinas, too, the heart is the principal member of the body, by which all the others are moved (*On Princely Government*, I.i and I.ii, 4 and 7). From the same work it is clear that the 'end' of human intention is the *bonum commune*. Members of the body politic 'intend' or are 'intent on' the common weal, to which they are directed by the light of reason (*On Princely Government* I.i and I.v, 2 and 13). But it is in Aquinas' analysis of human action in *Summa Theologica* that we can clearly see the point of the distinction between intention and will: intention means 'in aliud tendere', a striving for or desiring something. This desire cannot manifest as action until there has been some deliberation about the possible means to the end that is desired. Following a process of deliberation and consent, the individual can act. The final action is an act of choice which is an act of will (*voluntas*). Importantly, it is the intention which determines both the end and the legitimacy of the action

---

[24] Genet, *Four English Political Tracts*, pp. 119, 193.

of the will (Aquinas, *Summa Theologica*, Ia IIae qus.12 and 19). This language of 'intending the common good' is present in Aquinas' *On Princely Government* (I.v 13 and I.xv, 40–1) and it is also to be found in works contemporary with Fortescue, notably the *Boke of Noblesse* and the *Somnium Vigilantis*.

Thus it is the intention of the people which is the prime motivation in the setting up of the political kingdom, just as it is the heart which first moves and gives life to the physical body. In the process of incorporation, the political kingdom acquires a king in the same way that the body 'grows' a head. The fully-formed body politic then acts (as does the physical body) through its will. The aim or end of its actions and the touchstone for the legitimacy of those actions is the intention of the people, the intention that their lives and goods should be protected by the king who has been given tutelage of the realm. The means of protection and justice is the law. This can be clearly seen in the following passage:

> The law (*lex*), indeed, by which a group of men (*cetus hominum*) is made into a people (*populus*), resembles the sinews of the body physical, for, just as the body is held together by the sinews, so this body mystical is bound together and united into one by the law, which is derived from 'ligando', and the members and bones of this body, which signify the solid basis of truth by which the community is sustained, preserve their rights through the law, as the body natural does through the sinews.
>
> (*Praise*, ch.XIII. I have changed Chrimes' translation
> of '*nervi*' from 'nerves' to 'sinews').

The law is what binds the body politic together and through which its members preserve their rights; Fortescue elsewhere uses the phrase 'a bond of right (*vinculum iuris*)' to define law (*Nature*, I.xxx), the literal meaning of 'vinculum' being the rope used to lash a ship together which thus fits well with the notion of 'gubernatio' as the steering of a ship. The motive for the act of self-incorporation is the protection of life and goods. This aim would be frustrated if the very person whom they had set up could then take everything away from them (*Praise*, ch.XIV p. 23); hence the king cannot change the laws without the consent of his people any more than the head can change the body's sinews (*Praise*, ch.XIII p. 21). The Chancellor concludes:

You have here, Prince, the form of the institution of the political kingdom, whence you can estimate the power that the king can exercise in respect of the law and the subjects of such a realm; for a king of this sort is obliged to protect (*ad tutelam erectus est*) the law, the subjects, their bodies and goods, and he has power to this end issuing from the people (*a populo effluxam*), so that it is not possible for him to rule his people with any other power.

(*Praise*, ch.XIII)

The people 'intends' the *utilitas publicum*, that is, the protection of their lives and goods, their interests, justice, the common weal, and it is to this end that the king has power from the people. The flow of power (like the flow of blood) is from the heart to the head in and for the interest of the whole body. This is what is meant by the participation of many in government by one. There is no sense of opposition, no real duality at all, because the body politic is a single organism. The rule of law is a co-operative and corporate matter which must involve the intention, deliberation and consent of all members of the body politic, including the king, but which cannot be manifested as action without the single will of the king. In the establishment of a political kingdom the people do not hand everything over to the discretion of the king and they continue to make their intentions known in the representative and consultative bodies of the realm – parliament and the council. Government is a public concern.

There are many clear advantages to the English system according to Fortescue. First, there is the fact that the king becomes *character angelicus*; as king, he does not have the capacity or power to sin, he has his power for good and good alone, good being defined as the common good. This is a very significant part of Fortescue's theory; it is important that the 'political' nature of the monarchy should not be seen to reduce the power of the king or to place limitations on it, therefore Fortescue employs the notion of 'non-power' or 'impotence'. Power to sin is not power but impotence, therefore the king's inability to err, makes him more divine than human, he is perfectly free and all-powerful (*Praise*, ch.XIV, p. 24; *Governance*, chs.6 and 19, pp. 95, 122; *Nature*, Appendix A). Secondly, the king's provision of justice is better in a 'dominium politicum et regale' because the people receive 'such justice as they desire themselves' (*Governance*, ch.2, p. 87), and thirdly, the king always works for the common good because he is constrained thereto by the political law (*Praise*, ch.IX, p. 18). Fortescue states that because (as Aquinas says), 'the king is given for the kingdom and not the kingdom for the sake of the king' (*Praise*, ch.XXXVII, p. 53; pseudo-Aquinas, *De Regimine Principum*, III. iii),

> hence all the power of a king (*potestas regis*) ought to be applied to the good of his realm, which in effect consists in the defence of it against invasions by foreigners, and the protection of the inhabitants of the realm and their goods from injuries and rapine by natives.
>
> (*Praise*, ch.XXXVII, p. 53).

A king who cannot achieve this level of protection 'is necessarily judged impotent'. But a king who is 'so overcome by his own passions or poverty that he cannot keep his hands from despoiling his subjects', 'ought to be called not only impotent but impotence itself and cannot be deemed free'. Whilst a king who can defend his people against the oppression of both others and himself,

> is free and powerful . . . for who can be more powerful and freer than he who is able to restrain not only others but also himself? The king ruling his people politically can and always does do this.
>
> (*Praise*, ch.XXXVII, p. 53).

In the context of the mid-century crisis of governance caused by the weak and incapacitated kingship of Henry VI, this looks to be far from complacent commentary; in the atmosphere in which it was finally presented to Edward IV, it could equally have been read as a warning.

The realm of England is a 'dominium politicum et regale', a political kingdom, a polity-centred kingship, which originated in consent, not force.[25] It is primarily contrasted with the civil law kingship of France (*The Governance*, ch.I, pp. 83–4). There, 'what pleases the prince has the force of law', whereas the law whereby the kings of England rule consists in customs and statutes, as well as natural law, and they are bound to its observance by their coron-

---

[25] *Praise*, chs. XII–XIII, pp. 12–23; *Governance*, ch.II, p. 87; a major reason for not mentioning the Norman Conquest is that it would entail acknowledging the establishment of authority by force. In Fortescue's own collection (Bodleian Rawlinson MS C.398) there is a copy of Rede's Chronicle in which the paragraph on the Norman Conquest has been scored through, fo. 29.

ation oath (*Praise*, ch.XXXIV, p. 48). The chapter on English customary law is perhaps the best known of the whole work; in it the Chancellor states that throughout the history of England, from the rule of the Britons, through that of the Romans, Saxons, Danes and Normans,

> the realm has been continuously ruled by the same customs as it is now, customs which, if they had not been the best, some of those kings would have changed for the sake of justice or by the impulse of caprice, and totally abolished them . . . [no other laws] are so rooted in antiquity. Hence there is no gainsaying nor legitimate doubt but that the customs of the English are not only good but the best.
>
> (Praise, ch.XVII, pp. 26–7).

This passage, more than any other, is responsible for the reputation of Fortescue from Edward Coke onwards and thence to the twentieth-century charges of smugness. Let us deal with the last sentence first. It must be read in conjunction with the preceding claim that England's laws are to be judged according to the standard of justice and their suitability for the realm (*Praise*, ch.XV, p. 25); English common law is 'the best' because it is best suited to the realm of England (*Praise*, ch.XXIX, p. 44 and Chrimes, 1942, ciii). Fortescue is not, however, saying that English laws are the best *because* they are the oldest; the fact that the laws of England are ancient and have survived so long intact, is *proof* that they are the best and most just laws, it is not the *reason* for their being so,[26] Fortescue states that they have not been changed because they have not needed to be changed 'for the sake of justice'. This is an attempt to play down all of the major constitutional upheavals of the realm in order to stress that the essence of English kingship has remained unchanged since its first institution by Brutus' band of Trojans; history is pulled into line behind an idealised notion of the constitution of the realm.

Some of the implications of Fortescue's combination of political and royal elements become clearer when we look at his understanding of statute law. In England, statutes 'are made not only by the prince's will, but also by the assent of the whole realm, so they cannot be injurious nor fail to secure their advantage' (*Praise*,

---

[26] *Pace* Pocock, *The Machiavellian Moment*, p. 15.

ch.XVIII, p. 27),[27] unlike laws in a 'dominium regale' which work against the subjects to the advantage of the prince. Statutes made in parliament, are 'necessarily replete with prudence and wisdom' because they are 'promulgated by the prudence ... of more than three hundred chosen men' (*Praise*, ch.XVIII, p. 27; cf. *Modus Tenendi Parlamentum*). Moreover, if they 'happen not to give full effect to the intention of the makers (*intencio conditorum*), they can speedily be revised, and yet not without the assent of the commons and nobles of the realm, in the manner in which they first originated' (*Praise*, ch.XVIII, p. 28).[28]

The *corpus mysticum* of the realm becomes visible, is physically represented, in time of parliament. The *universitas* makes the laws by which it is governed; this is self-government, a 'dominium politicum'. But members of the realm of England are subjects, not citizens,[29] and they are summoned to parliament by the will of the king; this is self-government at the king's command, a 'dominium politicum et regale'. However, the king himself is bound at his coronation to ensure that justice is done 'as often as equity requires it' (*Praise*, ch.LIII, p. 78; cf. *Nature* Clermont edn 1869, I.xxiv) and therefore England is 'always really or potentially governed by the most excellent laws' (*Praise*, ch.LIV, p. 78). It is in parliament that the body politic strives to actualise its potential by means of the law, hence 'all the laws of this realm are the best in fact or potentiality (*in actu vel potencia*), since they can easily be brought to it in fact and actual reality (*essenciam realem*)' (*Praise*, ch.LIII, p. 78).

The central sections of *Praise* are comparisons of the English and civil law systems on specific points of law and procedure and these are dealt with in the footnotes to the text. These chapters became a model for later writers, notably John Hales and Thomas Smith. Fortescue compares the private, summary justice meted out by the provosts of the marshals in France, the routine use of torture and the inadequacies and iniquities of witness procedure with an English system cleansed of all corruption, pride of place going to the unique trial by jury (*Praise*, chs.XXI–XXVIII, pp. 30–42). The main reason for the difference in procedure is the fertility of England and its

---

[27] Doe, *Fundamental Authority in Late Medieval English Law*.

[28] The commons were added to the formal assenting clause of statutes in 1444–5, McKenna, 'The Coronation Oil of the Yorkist Kings'.

[29] Burns, 'Fortescue and the Political Theory of *dominium*'.

county system (*Praise*, chs.XXIX–XXX, pp. 42–4), but the nature of the law of England is also due to the origin of the realm. Both *Praise* and *The Governance* contain passages contrasting the condition of the 'poor commons' of each realm (*Praise*, ch. XXXV–XXXVI, pp. 49–53; *Governance*, ch. 3, pp. 87–90), with the intention that 'by their fruits you shall know them' (*Governance*, ch. 3, p. 90). In France, the picture is one of abject poverty; there the people live under excessive tax burdens, they are not free to enjoy what they have, being constantly plundered by the king's men, they toil on the land, wander barefoot in sackcloth and eat no meat. The picture for England is an early presentation of England as the land of 'roast beef and liberty', where the people freely enjoy their goods, eat meat, wear woollens and where the land is so fertile it scarcely needs cultivation. These are the blessings of the land of the just and obedient contrasted with the curses of tyranny and disobedience (Deuteronomy 28).

In *Praise*, then, Fortescue argues for justice against tyranny, showing clearly that England is a political monarchy which functions according to the intentions of, or in the interests of, the people; the king is for the sake of the kingdom. The dangers of monarchy are manifold; with one person at the helm, the fundamental problems of human weakness are ever-present, such as the tendency to give in to one's passions. This would lead to tyranny; the seeking of private over public good. As we have seen, this can happen because of the lust and ambition (passions) of the king, or because of his poverty which compels him to seek beyond what is his own. The central theme of *The Governance* is the provision of safeguards against the poverty and hence potential tyranny of the king.

The poverty of the king was a constituent part of the crisis of governance as contemporaries saw it in the 1440s and 1450s. The debts and excessive gifts of Henry VI during that period[30] constitute the situation for which it was first drafted.[31] By the time it was

---

[30] Wolffe, *The Crown Lands*.

[31] Of the ten extant manuscripts of *The Governance*, two read 'Henry VI' in place of 'Edward IV' at chapter 19, one, whilst reading 'Edward IV', has an added note that the work was 'written to King Henry the Sixth', three stop short of chapter 19, and in one, the relevant passage is mutilated, leaving only three full copies addressed unequivocally to Edward IV, (Plummer edn, (1885), 87–94). Plummer believed that the manuscripts were altered 'to avoid shocking Tudor susceptibilit-

presented to Edward IV, however, it has been generally thought to have lost its first freshness – it has been labelled 'old hat' and 'a compound of stale and misguided advice'.[32] However, it was presented in an atmosphere of reform and money-saving, as evidenced among other things, by the *Black Book* of Edward IV.[33] The household reforms suggested by the *Black Book* and the ordinances of 1445 and 1478 were not only cost-cutting exercises, they were also intended to improve efficiency through reform of the officers.[34] In the parliament of 1467, Edward IV had stated his intention to 'live of his own' (*Rot. Parl.* v.572).[35] Given the reformist preoccupations of 1471, it is clear that Fortescue had not entirely missed the boat with his suggestions in *The Governance*. On the contrary, it was presumably well-received since he gained the return of his lands and a place on Edward's council.

The Governance begins with an account of the diversity of royal kingship and political and royal kingship and their effects. Fortescue then proceeds to elucidate 'the harm that comes of a king's poverty' (*Governance*, ch. 5, p. 92): poverty erodes 'the glory of the king' and 'there may no realm prosper or be worshipful under a poor king' (*The Governance*, ch. 5, p. 93). It is important that we see Fortescue's argument against the poverty of the king not simply in economic terms, but as a serious political issue; it involves the king's need to maintain his estate and dignity by offering not merely good lordship, but the best. The king must maintain his estate above that of those immediately below him, and must be able to reward service in order to secure it since 'the people will go with him that best may sustain and reward them' (*Governance*, ch. 9, p. 101). Fortescue's conclusion is that 'there may no greater peril grow to a prince than to have a subject equipollent to himself' (*Governance*, ch. 9, p. 103; cf. Ashby *Active Policy of a Prince*, ll.639–42). Given the poverty of Henry VI (at his 'readeption' in

---

ies', but it is more likely that the work was intended for Henry VI, that it underwent some changes before being presented to Edward IV, and that the manuscripts reflect the work's changing fortunes. Attempts to date the work from internal evidence are flawed by the likelihood of several editorial changes.

[32] Starkey, 'Which Age of Reform?' in C. Coleman and D. Starkey (eds.), *Revolution Reassessed*, p. 15; Wolffe, *The Crown Lands*, p. 27.

[33] Mertes, *The English Noble Household 1256–1600*.

[34] Myers, *The Household of Edward IV*.

[35] Wolffe, *The Crown Lands*, pp. 51–65.

1470, Henry's progress was said to be 'more like a play than the showing of a prince to win men's hearts . . . and ever he was shown in a long blue gown of velvet as though he had no more to change with', *Great Chronicle*, 215), and the threat to his position in the 1450s from the availability of alternatives (in particular Richard, duke of York), Fortescue's work reads as a critical warning and once presented to Edward IV it still appears as prudent advice. Moreover, there is a direct link between the economic welfare of the realm and its security:

> the greatest safety, truly, and also the most honour that may come to a king is that his realm be rich in every estate. For nothing may make his people to arise but lack of goods or lack of justice. But yet certainly when they lack goods they will arise, saying that they lack justice. Nevertheless, if they be not poor, they will never arise but if their prince so leaves justice that he gives himself all to tyranny.
>
> *(Governance*, ch. 12, p. 110)

Fortescue's solution to these problems consists in a resumption of Crown lands by act of parliament, a new foundation of the Crown with a perpetual endowment and a reformed standing council to administer gifts and distribute offices in the future. The idea of a resumption of Crown lands, together with a subsidy, was not original, certainly not by 1470 when there had already been several statutes.[36] The most unusual and challenging aspect of his reforms is the new foundation of the Crown. Once the king has recovered his livelihood, he shall then 'amortise the same livelihood to his crown, so that it may never be alienated therefrom, without the assent of his parliament, which would then be a new foundation of his crown' (*Governance*, ch. 19, p. 121). In this way, the king shall have 'founded a whole realm, and endowed it with greater possessions, and better than ever was any realm in Christendom'.

Fortescue expresses this conclusion by speaking of the realm as a 'college' (*Governance*, ch. 19, p. 122). This has been treated as a flight of fancy but it is in fact a coherent part of his theory. The idea of the realm as a *collegium* fits completely with the concept already noted of the king as tutor or guardian of the realm as public property since *collegia* were ecclesiastical bodies such as chapters

[36] Wolffe, *The Crown Lands.*

and congregations which were *universitates* or perpetual persons who were also minors in need of a guardian, such as a bishop.[37] Fortescue's idea of a college is that of a voluntary association in which lay and clerical are joined together, represented by the abstract notion of the Crown.

We can now see *The Governance* as a serious attempt to protect, preserve and conserve the *bonum commune*, the *res publica*, in the sense of the rights, personal and real, of the members of the realm, including the king. It constitutes a strengthening of the public sphere and is therefore another bulwark against tyranny. This is also the purpose of the conciliar reforms suggested in *The Governance*.

The king's council was concerned with the regulation of the operation of the will of the king; the king needed to be able to make an informed and dispassionate choice – 'thy counsel take of them that can thee direct by politic wisdom in each moving, habit or passion, thee to reduce by good discretion' (Lydgate and Burgh, *Secrees of Old Philisoffres*, 11.2173–77; cf. Genet, *Four Political Tracts*, 194–5 and Ashby, *Active Policy of a Prince*, 11.359–60). The council is to assist the king in the deliberation of policy and in matters concerning the administration of kingship (*Governance*, ch. 15, p. 116), for example, war, the money supply and the preparation of legislation for parliament. The subject of counsel is a commonplace of advice-book literature – 'ubi multi consilia, ibi salus' (*Governance*, ch. 14, p. 114) – but Fortescue breaks away from the traditional claim that the nobility are the king's 'natural counsellors (*consiliarii nati*)'. Fortescue's council is not to be solely, or even primarily, of the lords of the realm, but of men chosen on merit for their wisdom, experience and expertise (*Governance*, ch. 15, p. 115).[38] Indeed, it is in keeping with Fortescue's general antipathy to the exclusive influence of the nobility that he makes no mention of the great councils which were exclusively noble assemblies, summoned to deliberate on matters of great importance.

Into his discussion of the council and its duties, Fortescue inserts a chapter about the senate of Rome (*Governance*, ch. 16, p. 117). This rather sparse account may be supplemented by reference to his 'Example of what good counsel helps and advantages and of the

---

[37] Kantorowicz, *The King's Two Bodies*.
[38] Guy 'The King's Council and Political Participation' in A. Fox and J. Guy, *Reassessing the Henrician Age*.

contrary what follows' (Appendix B). The analogy with Rome is intended to be loose; it is a statement of the value of the rule of one by the advice of many and it asserts the preference for public over private counsel. The relevance to England of this advice is made clear – non-elected, private counsellors have caused poverty, decay and civil war – 'since our kings have been ruled by private counsellors, such as have offered their service and counsel, and were not chosen thereto, we have not been able to keep our own livelihood . . . [this has caused] civil wars amongst ourselves . . . and our realm is fallen thereby into decay and poverty' ('Example', Appendix B). The nobility

> had almost as many matters of their own to be treated in the council, as had the king. Wherefore, when they came together, they were so occupied with their own matters, and with the matters of their kin, servants and tenants that they attended but little, and other whiles nothing, to the king's matters.
>
> (*Governance*, ch.15, p. 114)

Fortescue recommends his council because it will be both more efficient and more economical. It is to restrain the king in the giving away of land, offices, corrodies and pensions, such that

> his offices shall then be given to such as shall only serve him. Wherefore he shall have then a greater might and protection of his officers, when he wishes to call them, than he now has of his other feedmen under the estate of lords.
>
> (*Governance*, ch.17, p. 118)

Each man, from chancellor to park keeper, shall have only one office and therefore shall serve only the king (the exceptions to this being the king's brothers and those who 'serve the king about his person' who may hold two offices): 'forsooth it is not easily estimable, what might the king may have of his officers, if each of them had but one office, and served no other man but the king' (*Governance*, ch.17, p. 118). This has been seen as far-fetched and misguided[39] but an attempt was also made to do something like it under Henry V when confirmations of offices and annuities granted by the king were invariably made on condition that the recipient was retained by no

---

[39] Horrox, *Richard III; a Study of Service*, p. 315.

one other than the king.[40] Members of the *res publica* are expected to serve the common weal by holding office according to their ability and expertise, these offices are therefore for term of life only. Office-holders thus serve the common weal by serving the king, of whom they hold office and to whom they are sworn subjects.

We must not leave *The Governance* without saying something about the very last line: Fortescue says of the king, 'and yet he may leave this order when he wishes'. This has been interpreted either as a last-minute throw-away line to pacify Edward IV or as a serious and puzzling undermining of the political nature of English kingship for which Fortescue had apparently been establishing a case. Given the admonitory nature of the work, there is even perhaps an ironic tone to the words: the king, as an individual, has free will and he therefore has the capacity to do whatever he wishes, but the whole force of the work is that if he fails to take the advice, he will be acting according to his own passions and private welfare and not for the good of the realm. He will not be acting to fulfil the intentions of his people.

As has been shown, the attainment of justice and the common weal by the body politic of the realm is dependent on the right orientation of the king's will to the intention of the people. Fortescue goes as far as he can (without splitting a single organism into two) in showing that much of the steering towards the end of good governance is to be done on the advice of and with the consent of the people. Governance is shared because it cannot be divided. However, Fortescue will not forfeit the unity which is the value of monarchy and therefore there is ultimately only one pair of hands at the helm; the subjects cannot participate in governance unless and until they are summoned to do so by the will of the king to which they are subject.

In conclusion, therefore, Fortescue's political thought represents to a large extent the 'Englishing' of Thomist theory – much of the terminology and concepts are derived from *On Princely Government* and its continuation by Ptolemy of Lucca, but they are combined with and applied to the theory and practice of English common law and the institutions of the realm, especially parliament. The political aspects of 'dominium politicum et regale' are institutionalised in

---

[40] Bean, *The Decline of English Feudalism*, p. 210.

parliament and council, but these are institutions summoned by and subject to the will of the king. The body cannot act without the will of the king, but the king cannot rule rightly unless he follows the intention of the people. The representation of the shared, public aspects of the body politic is the Crown which is protected by the king as guardian and which has the rights and protection of a minor. The king is *tutor regni*, but by definition, only when he acts in its interest for the *bonum commune*, for the *res publica*. The political king 'can and always does do this' because he is restrained by political law, law made by king and people in parliament (*Praise*, ch.IX, p. 18). There is, therefore, no duality,[41] in his political thought; the king rules politically in a single body politic. King and people are bound together by the *vinculum iuris* and together they deliberate and determine the means to their single destination.

---

[41] *Pace* Hanson, *From Kingdom to Commonwealth*, p. 218.

Principal events in Fortescue's life

c. 1395	Born at Norris in Devon
1399 October	Accession of Henry IV
1413 March	Accession of Henry V
Before 1420	Admitted to Lincoln's Inn
1420 May	Treaty of Troyes
1422 August	Henry V dies at Vincennes and Henry VI, aged nine months, succeeds him. He is king of England and heir to the crown of France
October	Charles VI of France dies and Henry VI becomes king of England and of France. John, duke of Bedford and Humphrey, duke of Gloucester are made protectors
Before 1423	Marries Elizabeth Brytte
1424–6 and 1428–9	Governor of Lincoln's Inn
1429–30	Pensioner and Governor of Lincoln's Inn
1429 November	Coronation of Henry VI at Westminster and the end of the protectorate of Bedford and Gloucester
1430	Serjeant-at-law
1431	Coronation of Henry VI at Paris
Before 1436	Marries Isabella Jamyss
1437	Henry VI comes of age
1441	King's serjeant
1442 January	Chief Justice of the King's Bench
1443	Knighted

1444		Truce of Tours
1445		Henry VI marries Margaret of Anjou
1447	February	Death of Humphrey, duke of Gloucester
	April	Death of Cardinal Beaufort
1448		Surrender of Anjou and Maine
1450	January	Trial of William de la Pole, earl of Suffolk
	April	Battle of Formigny: loss of Normandy
	May	Suffolk beheaded by rebels
		Jack Cade's rebellion
	July	Battle of Castillon: loss of Guyenne
1453	August	Henry VI collapses
	October	Birth of Prince Edward
1454	March–	
	February 1455	First protectorate of Richard, duke of York
	March	First battle of St Albans
	November–	Second protectorate of Richard, duke of
	February 1456	York
1459	September	Battle of Blore Heath
	November	'Parliament of Devils' at Coventry
	December	Attainder of the Yorkists
1460	July	Battle of Northampton: Henry is captured, Queen Margaret and Prince Edward flee north
	October	Richard, duke of York claims the throne
	December	Battle of Wakefield: Richard, duke of York is killed
1461	February	Battle of Mortimer's Cross
		Second battle of St Albans: Margaret recaptures Henry
	March	Edward IV proclaimed king
		Battle of Towton (Fortescue present)
		Henry, Margaret and Prince Edward flee to Edinburgh
	June	Coronation of Edward IV
		Fortescue joins Henry, Margaret and Prince Edward in Edinburgh
	July	
	(to July 1463)	Whilst in Scotland Fortescue writes *De Titulo Edwardi Comitis Marchiae*, 'On the

title of the House of York', *Defensio Juris Domus Lancastriae*, 'A Defence of the title of the House of Lancaster, or a Replication to the claim of the Duke of York' and *Opusculum de Natura Legis Naturae et eius Censura in Successione Regnorum Suprema*

Fortescue is nominal chancellor to Henry

December	Fortescue is attainted
1463 July	To St Mihiel in Bar, France, with Queen Margaret and Prince Edward
1464	
Before December	Fortescue visits Paris
Between 1468 and 1471	Fortescue, whilst still in France, writes *De laudibus legum Anglie*
1469	
July to September	Earl of Warwick keeps Edward IV in confinement
1470 April	Earl of Warwick flees to France
?May	Fortescue summoned with Queen Margaret to Paris by Louis XI
	Fortescue writes 'Memoranda on the political situation' for Louis XI
?August	Fortescue participates in negotiations with the earl of Warwick and Louis XI at Angers
September	Earl of Warwick invades and Edward IV flees to Holland
?November	Fortescue writes 'Articles from Prince Edward to the Earl of Warwick'
Before 1471	Fortescue possibly translates the works of Alain Chartier
1471 March	Edward IV lands at Ravenspur
April	Fortescue lands at Weymouth with Margaret and Prince Edward
	Battle of Barnet: earl of Warwick is killed, Henry VI is captured and placed in the Tower
May	Battle of Tewkesbury: Prince Edward is killed, Fortescue and Margaret are captured
	Henry dies (murdered) in the Tower

October	Fortescue writes 'Declaration upon Certain Writings sent out of Scotland'
	Fortescue is pardoned, becomes a member of Edward IV's council and presents him with a copy of *The Governance of England*
1475 February	Fortescue obtains a reversal of his attainder
c 1477	Fortescue dies and is buried in Ebrington church, Gloucestershire

Select bibliography

Primary sources

Gairdner, J. (ed.) *Three Fifteenth-Century Chronicles* (Camden Soc. n.s. 28, London, 1880)

Genet, J-P. (ed.) *Four English Political Tracts of the later Middle Ages* (Camden Soc. 4th ser. vol.18, London, 1977)

Kail, J. (ed.) *26 Political and Other Poems* (EETS o.s. 124 London, 1904)

Aquinas, Thomas *Summa Theologica*, ed. T. Gilby *et al.*, 61 vols. (Blackfriars, 1964–1980)

'On Princely Government' Book I in A.P. D'Entreves (ed.) *Selected Political Writings* (Oxford, 1948)

pseudo-Aquinas *De Regimine Principum* in J. Perrier (ed.) *Opuscula Omnia Necnon Opera Minora* vol. I *Opera Philosophica* (Paris, 1949) App.I. This was Ptolemy of Lucca, Aquinas' continuator

Aristotle *The Politics* ed. S. Everson, (Cambridge, 1988)

Nicomachean Ethics ed. J. Barnes, (Penguin Classics, London, 1976)

pseudo-Aristotle *Liber de Causis* ed. A. Pattin in *Tijdschrift voor Filosofie* 28 (1966), 90–203

Secreta Secretorum ed. M.A. Manzalaoui (EETS, Oxford, 1977)

Auctoritates Aristotelis ed. J. Hamesse (Louvain, 1974)

Ashby, George *Active Policy of a Prince* ed. M. Bateson (EETS, London, 1899)

Augustine *The City of God* (Loeb edn, London, 1960)

The Black Book of Edward IV (Liber Niger) in A.R. Myers (ed.) *The Household of Edward IV* (Manchester, 1959)

Boethius *The Consolation of Philosophy* (Penguin Classics, London, 1969)

de Bracton, Henri *On the Laws and Customs of England* ed. G.E. Woodbine, trans. S.E. Thorne (4 vols., Cambridge, Mass., 1968)

Bruni, Leonardo 'Isagogue of Moral Philosophy' in H. Baron (ed.), *Humanistisch-Philosophische Schriften* (Berlin, 1928), 20–41 and trans. in G. Griffiths et al. (eds.), *The Humanism of Leonardo Bruni* (New York, 1987), 267–82

Chartier, Alain *A Familiar Dialogue of the Friend and the Fellow*, ed. M.S. Blayney (EETS, Oxford, 1989)

Fifteenth-Century Translations of Alain Chartier's Le Traité de L'Espérance and Le Quadrilogue Invectif, ed. M.S. Blayney (EETS, Oxford, 1974)

Cicero *De Re Publica* (Loeb edn, London, 1928)

Code See under Justinian

Corpus Iuris Canonici See under Gratian

de Commynes, Philippe *Memoirs of the Reign of Louis XI 1461–1483* ed. M. Jones (Penguin Classics, London, 1972)

Dictes and Sayinges of Philosophers ed. C.F. Buhler (EETS, London, 1941)

Digest See under Justinian

Diodorus Siculus *Library of History, De Priscis Historiis (Ancient Histories)* ed. F.M. Salter and H.L.K. Edwards (EETS, London, 1956)

Elyot, Thomas *The Boke Named the Governor* ed. S.E. Lehmberg (1962)

'The Image of Gouernaunce' in L. Gottesmann (ed.), *Four Political Treatises . . . by Sir Thomas Elyot* (Florida, 1967), 203–462

An English Chronicle of the reigns of Richard II, Henry IV, Henry V and Henry VI written before the year 1471, ed. J.S. Davies (Camden Soc., London, 1856)

FitzNigel, Richard *Dialogue of the Exchequer* ed. C. Johnson (Oxford, 1983)

Fortescue, John *The Works of Sir John Fortescue* ed. Lord Clermont (London, 1869)

Containing:

'De Titulo Edwardi Comitis Marchiae', 63*–90*

'Of the Title of the House of York' 497–502
'Defensio Juris Domus Lancastriae' 505–16
'A Defence of the Title of the House of Lancaster, Or a Replication to the Claim of the Duke of York', 517–18
'Opusculum de Natura Legis Naturae, et de ejus Censura in Successione Regnorum Suprema', 60–184

E. Whitchurche, *Prenobilis militis cognomento Forescu . . . de politica administratione; et legibus civilibus florentissimi regni Anglie commentarius* (?1545)
R. Mulcaster, *A learned commendation of the politique lawes of Englande, wherein by most pithy reasons and evident demonstrations they are plainly proved farre to excell as well as the civile lawes of the Empiere, as also all other lawes of the world, with a large discourse on the difference between the II governements of kingdomes; whereof the one is onely regall, and the other consisteth of regall and politique conioyned . . .* (1567), (facsimile edn Amsterdam, 1969)
John Selden, *De laudibis legum Anglie* (1616)
De laudibus legum Anglie ed. S. B. Chrimes (Cambridge, 1942)
The difference between an absolute and a limited Monarchy; as it more particularly regards the English Constitution; being a treatise written by Sir John Fortescue, Knight, Lord Chief Justice and Lord High Chancellor under King Henry VI (London, 1714)
The Governance of England ed. C. Plummer (Oxford, 1885)
Containing:
'Example of what good counseill' 347–8
'Articles to the Earl of Warwick' 348–53
Geoffrey of Monmouth *History of the Kings of Britain* ed. L. Thorpe (Penguin Classics, London, 1966)
Giles of Rome *De Regimine Principum*, (On Princely Government) see G. Bruni, "De Regimine Principum" di Egidio Romano', *Aevum* VI (1932), 339–73
Gratian *Decretum, distinctio 1*, in A. Friedberg (ed.) *Corpus Iuris Canonici pars prior: Decretum Magistri Gratiani* (Graz, 1959)
Decretal Gregor IX, lib. IV, tit. 1, cap. XVIII, in A. Friedberg (ed.) *Corpus Iuris Canonici pars secunda: Decretalium Collectiones* (Graz, 1959)
The Great Chronicle of London, ed. A. H. Thomas and I. D. Thornley (London, 1938)

Hales, John, 'Oration in Commendation of the Laws, chiefly of the Laws of this most noble Realm of England' (*c.* 1541), British Library Harleian MS 4990, fos 1–48

Hake, Edward, *EPIEKEIA: A Dialogue on Equity in Three Parts* ed. D. E. C. Yale (Newhaven, Conn., 1953)

Institutes See under Justinian

Jacobus de Cessolis *Game of Chess Moralised* ed. F. Vetter (2 vols., Frauenfeld, 1892)

John of Salisbury *Policraticus* ed. C. C. J. Webb (2 vols., Oxford, 1909) and trans. and abridged C. J. Nederman (ed.) (Cambridge, 1990)

Justinian *Corpus Iuris Civilis*, 3 volumes:

Vol. I *Institutiones, Digesta* (*Institutes, Digest*), ed. T. Mommsen and P. Kreuger (Frankfurt, 1970)

Vol. II *Codex Iustinianus* (*Code*), ed. P. Kreuger (Frankfurt 1970)

Vol. III *Novellae* (*Novels*), ed. R. Schoell (Frankfurt 1968). See also the following English translations:

The Digest of Justinian, ed. P. Kreuger, T. Mommsen and A. Watson (Philadelphia, 1986)

The Institutes of Justinian, ed. J. A. C. Thomas (Cape Town, 1975)

Littleton, Thomas *Tenures* ed. E. Wambaugh (Washington, 1903)

Lydgate and Burgh *Secrees of Old Philisoffres* ed. R. Steele (EETS, London, 1894)

Modus Tenendi Parlamentum ed. N. Pronay and J. Taylor, *Parliamentary Texts of the later Middle Ages* (Oxford, 1980)

Novels See under Justinian

The Paston Letters ed. J. Gairdner (Gloucester, 1983)

Sir John Paston's Grete Boke ed. G. A. Lester (Suffolk, 1984)

Pecock, Reginald *The Repressor of Over-much Blaming of the Clergy* ed. C. Babington (2 vols., London, 1860)

Ptolemy of Lucca (see pseudo-Aquinas)

Rastell, John *Libri Assisarum et Placita Coronae* (1514) STC 9599

Pastyme of People (1529) ed. A. J. Geritz (New York, 1985)

Smith, Thomas *De Republica Anglorum* ed. M. Dewar (Cambridge, 1982)

Somnium Vigilantis in J.P. Gilson, 'A Defence of the Proscription of the Yorkists in 1459', *EHR* 26 (1911), 512–25

Starkey, Thomas *Dialogue between Reginald Pole and Thomas Lupset* ed. T.F. Mayer (London, 1989)

St German, Christopher *A Dialogue between a Doctor and a Student* ed.
T.F.T. Plucknett and J.L. Barton (Selden Soc., London, 1974)
Answere to a Letter (1535) (facsimile edn, Amsterdam, 1973)
Vincent of Beauvais 'On the Moral Education of a Prince', Bodleian
MS c.398, fos 89–119
Worcester, William *The Boke of Noblesse* ed. J.G. Nichols (London,
1860)

Secondary works

Historical background

Baker, J.H. *The Reports of Sir John Spelman* (Selden Soc., London,
1978)
The Order of the Serjeants-at-Law (Selden Soc., London, 1984)
The Legal Profession and the Common Law. Historical Essays (London,
1986)
Baldwin, J.F. *The King's Council in England During the Middle Ages*
(repr. Oxford, 1969)
Bean, J.M.W. *The Decline of English Feudalism 1215–1540* (New York,
1968)
From lord to patron: lordship in late medieval England (Manchester,
1989)
Bellamy, J.G. *The Law of Treason in England in the Middle Ages*
(Cambridge, 1970)
Criminal Law and Society in Late Medieval and Tudor England
(Gloucester, 1984)
Bastard Feudalism and the Law (London, 1989)
Bolton, J.L. *The Medieval English Economy 1150–1500* (London, 1980)
Brooke, C. and Sharpe, K. 'Debate: History, English Law and the
Renaissance', *Past and Present* 72 (1976), 133–42
Carpenter, C. *Locality and Polity: a Study of Warwickshire Landed
Society, 1401–1499* (Cambridge, 1992)
Carpenter, M.C. 'The Beauchamp Affinity: a study of bastard feudal-
ism at work', *EHR* (1980), 514–32
Clough, C.H. (ed.) *Profession, Vocation and Culture in Late Medieval
England* (Liverpool, 1982)
Cobban, A.B. *The Medieval English Universities: Oxford and Cambridge
to c. 1500* (Cambridge, 1988)

Crook, D.R. *Lancastrians and Yorkists: The Wars of the Roses* (London, 1984)

Dyer, C. *Standards of Living in the Later Middle Ages* (Cambridge, 1989)

Edwards, J.G. 'The *Plena Potestas* of English Parliamentary Representatives' in F.W. Powicke (ed.), *Oxford Essays Presented to H.E. Salter*, (Oxford, 1934) 141–54

Elton, G.R. *England 1200–1640* (Cambridge, 1977)

Fox, A. and Guy, J. *Reassessing the Henrician Age: Humanism, Politics and Reform 1500–1550* (Oxford, 1986)

Gaussin, P-R. *Louis XI Roi Méconnu* (Paris, 1976)

Goodman, A. *The New Monarchy; England 1471–1534* (Oxford, 1988)

Grant, A. *Independence and Nationhood; Scotland 1306–1469* (Edinburgh, 1984)

Gray, H.L. *The Influence of the Commons on Early Legislation. A Study of the Fourteenth and Fifteenth Centuries*, (Cambridge Mass., 1932)

Griffiths, R.A. *The Reign of Henry VI* (London, 1981)

Guenée, B. *States and Rulers in Later Medieval Europe* (London, 1985)

Harvey, I.M.H. *Jack Cade's Rebellion of 1450* (Oxford, 1991)

Heath, J. *Torture and English Law. An Administrative and Legal History from the Plantagenets to the Stuarts* (London, 1982)

Holt, J.C. *Magna Carta and Medieval Government* (London, 1985)

Horrox, R. *Richard III; a Study of Service* (Cambridge, 1989)

Horrox, R. (ed.) *Fifteenth Century Attitudes: Perceptions of Society in Late Medieval England* (Cambridge, 1994)

Ives, E.W. *The Common-Lawyers of Pre-Reformation England* (Cambridge, 1983)

Jacob, E.F. *The Fifteenth Century 1399–1485* (Oxford, 1961), (Repr. with corrections (Oxford, 1969))

Kekewich, M. 'The Attainder of the Yorkists in 1459: 2 Contemporary Accounts', *BIHR*, LV (1982), 25–34

Lander, J.R. *Conflict and Stability in Fifteenth-Century England* (3rd edn, London, 1977)

Lewis, P.S. (ed.) *The Recovery of France in the Fifteenth Century* (London, 1971)

Loades, D.M. *Politics and the Nation 1450–1660* (2nd edn, Glasgow, 1979)

MacFarlane, K.B. *England in the Fifteenth Century. Collected Essays* (London, 1981)

McKenna, J.W. 'The Coronation Oil of the Yorkist Kings' *EHR* 82 (1967), 102–4

Mertes, K. *The English Noble Household 1250–1600: Good Governance and Politic Rule* (Oxford, 1988)

Myers, A.R. *Crown, Household and Parliament in Fifteenth-Century England* (London, 1985)

Plucknett, T.F.T. 'Some Proposed Legislation of Henry VIII', *TRHS* 4th series XIX (1936), 119–44

A Concise History of the Common Law (5th edn, London, 1956)

Powell, E. *Kingship, Law and Society. Criminal Justice in the Reign of Henry V* (Oxford, 1989)

Roskell, J.S. *Parliament and Politics in Late Medieval England* (vol. 1, London, 1981)

Ross, C. *Edward IV* (London, 1974)

Schramm, P.E. *A History of the English Coronation* (Oxford, 1937)

Shennan, J.H. *Government and Society in France 1461–1661* (London, 1969)

Starkey, D. 'Which Age of Reform?' in C. Coleman and D. Starkey, (eds.) *Revolution Reassessed. Revisions in the History of Tudor Government and Administration* (Oxford, 1986), 13–27

Thomson, J.A.F. *The Transformation of Medieval England 1370–1529* (London, 1983)

Watts, J.L. *Henry VI and the Politics of Kingship* (Cambridge, 1996)

Wolffe, B.P. *The Crown Lands 1461–1536: An Aspect of Yorkist and Early Tudor Government* (London, 1969)

Henry VI (London, 1981)

Intellectual background

Bloch, M. *The Royal Touch. Sacred Monarchy and Scrofula in England and France* (London, 1973)

Burns, J.H. *The Cambridge History of Medieval Political Thought c.350–c.1450* (Cambridge, 1988)

The Cambridge History of Political Thought 1450–1700 (Cambridge, 1991)

Lordship, Kingship and Empire. The Idea of Monarchy 1400–1525 (Oxford, 1992)

Chrimes, S.B. *English Constitutional Ideas in the Fifteenth Century* (Cambridge, 1936)

Doe, N. *Fundamental Authority in Late Medieval English Law* (Cambridge, 1990)

Genet, J-P. 'Droit et Histoire en Angleterre: la préhistoire de la "révolution historique"', *Annales de Bretagne et des Pays de l'Ouest* LXXXVII (1980), 319–66

'Ecclesiastics and Political Theory in Late Medieval England: The End of a Monopoly' in R.B. Dobson ed., *The Church, Patronage and Politics in the Fifteenth Century* (Gloucester, 1984)

Green, R.F. *Poets and Prince Pleasers. Literature and the English Court in the late Middle Ages* (Toronto, 1980)

Hanson, D.W. *From Kingdom to Commonwealth; The Development of English Civic Consciousness in English Political Thought* (Cambridge, Mass., 1970)

Kantorowicz, E.H. *The King's Two Bodies A Study in Medieval Political Theology* (Princeton, 1957)

Kelley, D. 'History, English Law and the Renaissance', *Past and Present* 64 (1973), 24–51

Kingsford, C.L. *English Historical Literature in the Fifteenth Century* (Oxford, 1913)

Maitland, F.W. *Selected Passages from the Work of Bracton and Azo*, (London, 1895)

McIlwain, C.H. *The Growth of Political Thought in the West* (London, 1932)

Mitchell, R.J. *John Tiptoft (1427–1470)* (London, 1938)

Patrough, J.F. *Reginald Pecock* (New York, 1970)

Plucknett, T.F.T. *Early English Legal Literature* (Cambridge, 1958)

Pronay, N. and Taylor, J. 'The Use of the *Modus Tenendi Parlamentum* in the Middle Ages' *BIHR* 47 (1974), 11–23

Rubinstein, N. 'The history of the word *politicus* in early modern Europe' in A. Pagden (ed.), *The Languages of Political Theory in Early-Modern Europe* (Cambridge, 1987), 41–56

Scattergood, V.J. *Politics and Poetry in the Fifteenth Century* (London, 1971)

Seipp, D.J. 'Roman Legal Categories in Early Common Law' in T.G. Watkin (ed.), *Legal Record and Historical Reality* (London, 1989), 9–36

Stein, P.G. *Regulae Iuris. From Juristic Rules to Legal Maxims* (Edinburgh, 1966)

Viroli, M. *From Politics to Reason of State. The acquisition and transformation of the language of politics 1250–1600* (Cambridge, 1992)

Weiss, R. *Humanism in England during the Fifteenth Century* (Oxford, 1941)

Fortescue and his legacy

Blayney, M.S. 'Sir John Fortescue and Alain Chartier's "Traité de l'Espérance" ', *Modern Language Review* XLVIII (1953), 385–90

Burgess, G. *The Politics of the Ancient Constitution: an Introduction to English Political Thought 1603–1642* (London, 1992)

Burns, J.H. 'Fortescue and the Political Theory of *dominium*', *HJ* 28 (1985), 777–97

Christianson, P. 'John Selden, the Five Knights' Case and Discretionary Imprisonment in Early Stuart England', *Criminal Justice History* 6 (1985), 65–87

Collinson, P. 'The Monarchical Republic of Queen Elizabeth I', *Bulletin of the John Rylands Library* 69 (1987), 394–424

Doe, N. 'Fifteenth-century concepts of law: Fortescue and Pecock', *HPT* 10 (1989), 257–80

Ferguson, A.B. 'Fortescue and the Renaissance: a Study in Transition', *Studies in the Renaissance* VI (1959), 175–94

Geritz, A.J. and Laine, A.L. *John Rastell* (Boston, 1983)

Gilbert, F. 'Sir John Fortescue's "dominium regale et politicum" ', *Medievalia et Humanistica* II (1944), 88–97

Gill, P.E. 'Politics and Propaganda in Fifteenth-Century England: the Polemical Writings of Sir John Fortescue', *Speculum* 46 (1971), 333–47

Gillespie, J.L. 'Sir John Fortescue's Concept of Royal Will', *Nottingham Medieval Studies* XXIII (1979), 47–65

Guy, J. 'The King's Council and Political Participation' in A. Fox and J. Guy, *Reassessing the Henrician Age* (Oxford, 1986), 121–47

Litzen, V. *A War of Roses and Lilies: The Theme of Succession in Sir John Fortescue's Works* (Helsinki, 1971)

Mendle, M. 'Parliamentary sovereignty: a very English absolutism' in N. Phillipson and Q. Skinner (eds), *Political discourse in early modern Britain* (Cambridge, 1993), 97–119

Mosse, G.L. 'Sir John Fortescue and the Problem of Papal Power', *Medievalia et Humanistica* VII (1952), 89–94

Pocock, J.G.A. *The Machiavellian Moment* (Princeton, 1975)

The Ancient Constitution and the Feudal Law. A Study of English Historical Thought in the Seventeenth Century. A Reissue with a Retrospect (Cambridge, 1987)

'A discourse on sovereignty: observations on work in progress' in Phillipson and Skinner (eds), *Political discourse in early modern Britain* (Cambridge, 1993), 377–428

Skeel, C.A. 'The Influence of the Writings of Sir John Fortescue', *TRHS*, 3rd series X (1916), 77–114

Sommerville, J.P. *Politics and Ideology in England 1603–1640* (London, 1986)

Abbreviations

BIHR	*Bulletin of the Institute of Historical Research*
CIC	*Corpus Iuris Civilis* of Justinian
EETS	Early English Text Society
EHR	*English Historical Review*
HJ	*Historical Journal*
HPT	*History of Political Thought*
PL	*Paston Letters* ed. J. Gairdner, reprinted with an introduction by Roger Virgoe (Gloucester, 1983)
PPC	*Proceedings of the Privy Council*
Rot. Parl.	*Rotuli Parliamentorum*, 7 vols. Edward I to Henry VII
STC	*A Short Title Catalogue of Books Printed in England, Scotland and Ireland and of English Books Printed Abroad*, ed. A.W. Pollard and G.R. Redgrave (2nd edition revised and enlarged by W.A. Jackson, F.S. Ferguson and K. Pantzer, 3 vols., London, 1986, 1976 and 1991)
TRHS	*Transactions of the Royal Historical Society*

In Praise of the
Laws of England

Introduction to the Matter

Not long ago, a savage and most detestable civil war raged in the kingdom of England, whereby Henry the Sixth, most pious king, with Margaret his queen-consort, daughter of the King of Jerusalem and Sicily, and their only son Edward, Prince of Wales, were driven out of the realm, and whereby King Henry was himself eventually seized by his subjects and for a long time suffered the horror of imprisonment. The Queen meanwhile, thus banished from the country with her child, lodged in the duchy of Bar in the domain of the said King of Jerusalem.[1]

The Prince, as soon as he became grown up, gave himself over entirely to martial exercises; and, seated on fierce and half-tamed steeds urged on by his spurs, he often delighted in striking and assailing the young companions attending him,[2] sometimes with a lance, sometimes with a sword, sometimes with other weapons, in a warlike manner and in accordance with the rules of military discipline. Observing this, a certain aged knight, chancellor of the said

Books mentioned in the footnotes which also appear in the *Select bibliography* are referred to by author and short title. Other books are given full details.

[1] This refers to the period of exile 1463–1471, see 'Principal events in Fortescue's life' and 'Select bibliography' above xl–xliii and xliv–liii.

[2] According to William Worcester there were some 200 people with the Queen at Bar, *Liber Niger Scaccarii, necnon William Worcesterii annales rarum Anglicarum*, II.ii, ed. T. Hearne, (2 vols., London, 1774). These included the dukes of Exeter and Somerset, Edmund Mundford, Edmund Hamden, Henry Roos, John Morton, William Vaux and Robert Whityngham.

King of England,[3] who was also in exile there as a result of the same disaster, thus addressed the prince.

Chapter I
Here the Chancellor first moves the Prince to the study of the law

'I do indeed rejoice, most fair Prince, at your noble disposition, perceiving as I do with how much eagerness you embrace military exercises, which are fitting for you to take such delight in, not merely because you are a knight but all the more because you are going to be king. "For the office of a king is to fight the battles of his people and to judge them rightfully", as you may very clearly learn in I Kings, chapter viii.[4] For that reason, I wish that I observed you to be devoted to the study of the laws with the same zeal as you are to that of arms, since, as battles are determined by arms, so judgements are by laws. This fact the Emperor Justinian carefully bears in mind when, in the beginning of the Preface to his book of *Institutes*, he says, "Imperial Majesty ought to be not only adorned with arms but also armed with laws, so that it can govern aright in both times of peace and of war."[5]

Furthermore, Moses, that greatest of legislators, leader of the synagogue in time past, invites you to strive zealously in the study of the law, even more forcefully than Caesar, when with divine authority he commands the kings of Israel to read their laws every day of their lives, saying thus, "After the king has sat on the throne of his kingdom, he shall write for himself the laws of Deuteronomy in a book, receiving a copy from the priests of the Levites, and he shall have it with him, and shall read it all the days of his life, so that he may learn to fear the Lord his God, and to keep His words

---

[3] Fortescue was possibly made Chancellor in 1461, but the official title could not have lasted more than two weeks. Henry VI, however, continued to refer to him as Chancellor.

[4] I Samuel 8:20. The four Books of Kings are I and II Samuel and I and II Kings.

[5] *CIC, Institutes*, proemium. Bracton, too, began his work *On the Laws and Customs of England* (*c*.1256), 'To rule well a king requires two things, arms and laws, that by them both times of war and of peace may rightly be ordered', (Woodbine, edn (trans. Thorne), 19). On Bracton's derivation of this and many other statements from the civilian Azo, see F.W. Maitland, *Select Passages from the works of Bracton and Azo* (London, 1895).

and His rites, which are written in the law" (Deuteronomy, chapter xvii).[6] Helynandus, expounding this text, said, "The prince, therefore, ought not to be ignorant of the law, nor is he permitted, on pretext of military duty, to be ignorant of it", and, a little further on, "he is commanded to receive a copy of the law from the priests of the Levites, that is, from men catholic and learned".[7] Thus says he.

The Book of Deuteronomy, indeed, is the book of the laws by which the kings of Israel were bound to rule the people subject to them. Moses commands the kings to read this book, so that they may learn to fear God and to keep His commandments, which are written in the law.[8] Lo! to fear God is the effect of the law, which man shall not be able to attain to unless he first knows the will of God, which is written in the law. For the beginning of all service is to know the will of the lord whom you serve. Yet Moses, giver of laws, mentions first in this command the effect of the law, namely the fear of God, and then exhorts to the observance of the cause thereof, namely the commandments of God; for the effect is prior to the cause in the mind of him who exhorts.

But what sort of fear is it that the laws promise to those who keep them? Truly, it is not that fear of which it is written that "Perfect love casts out fear."[9] Yet that fear, though it is abject, often incites kings to read the laws, but is not itself the offspring of the law. That fear, of which Moses here speaks and which the laws beget, is that of which the prophet says, "The fear of the Lord remains for ever holy."[10] This fear is as a son's for his father, and knows not the pain of that fear which is cast out by love. For this fear is promoted by the laws, which teach the doing of the will of God, by which we escape pain. "But the glory of the Lord is upon

---

[6] Deuteronomy 17:18–19.

[7] Helynandus (d.1219), *De Bono Regimine Principis*, printed in J.P. Migne, *Patrologia Cursus Completus* CCXII, Series Latina (Paris, 1857–66), 735–46. These quotes from Deuteronomy and from Helynandus are to be found in Vincent of Beauvais, *On the Moral Education of a Prince*, a copy of which is in Fortescue's own collection, Bodleian Rawlinson MS C.398, fo.106r.

[8] The account of the Mosaic law given in Deuteronomy is important to an understanding of Fortescue's concept of justice; the 'good things' and 'bad things' which come of the different forms of government in France and England are the blessings and curses of God, see below 49 and 51.

[9] I John 4:18.

[10] Psalms 19:9.

those that fear Him, whom also He glorifies."[11] This fear, further-more, is that of which Job, after he had sought wisdom in manifold ways, speaks thus, "Behold! fear of the Lord is wisdom itself, and to depart from evil is understanding" (Job, chapter xxviii).[12] The laws teach that departure from evil is understanding of the fear of God, whereby they also produce that fear.'

Chapter II
Replication of the Prince to the Chancellor's motion

When the Prince heard this, facing the old man squarely, he spoke thus, 'I know, Chancellor, that the Book of Deuteronomy which you mention is a book of holy scripture, and that the laws and usages set down therein are also sacred, decreed by the Lord and declared by Moses. For that reason it is good to read them with reverent thought. But the law, to a knowledge of which you exhort me, is human, decreed by man, and treats of this world; and, though Moses constrained the kings of Israel to the reading of Deu-teronomy,[13] nevertheless it is beyond all reason that he should have thereby obliged other kings to do the like with regard to their laws, since the purpose in studying the two sets of laws is not the same.'

Chapter III
Here the Chancellor strengthens his motion

'I know', the Chancellor said, 'from what you have just objected, Prince, with how much attention you consider the nature of my exhortation, whereby you encourage me not a little to discuss with you, up to a point, the matters that have been raised, not merely more clearly, but also more deeply. I want you, then, to know that not only the laws of Deuteronomy, but also all human laws, are sacred, inasmuch as law is defined by these words, "Law is a sacred sanction commanding what is honest and forbidding the con-trary."[14] For what is sacred by definition must be sacred. Law may

---

[11] Psalms 14:4.
[12] Job 28:28.
[13] Deuteronomy 17:18–19.
[14] This is from the Accursian gloss to *CIC Institutes*, I, 2, 3, V. *Lex*. Is is also in Bracton, Woodbine edn, 22, taken from Azo, *Summa Institutionum*, 1.1, no.4.

also be described as that which is the art of the good and the just, in virtue of which they call us priests.[15] For a priest is by etymology said to be one who gives or teaches holy things, and, because human laws are said to be sacred, hence the ministers and teachers of the laws are called priests.

Moreover, all laws that are promulgated by man are decreed by God. For, since the Apostle says "All power is from the Lord God",[16] laws established by man, who receives power to this end from God, are also formulated by God, as is implied by the Author of the Causes when he says that, "Whatever the second cause effects, so also does the first cause, in a sense superior and more excellent."[17] Wherefore, Jehoshaphat, King of Judah, says to his judges, "The judgements that you give are the judgements of God" (II Chronicles, chapter xix).[18] By this you are taught that to learn the laws, even though human ones, is to learn laws that are sacred and decreed of God, the study of which does not lack the blessing of divine encouragement.

But still, as you know, this blessing was not the reason that Moses commanded the kings of Israel to read Deuteronomy. For, on that account, he exhorted the kings no more than the people to the reading thereof, nor did he encourage the reading of the Book of Deuteronomy more than other books of the Pentateuch, since those books no less than Deuteronomy abound in revelations of the Holy Spirit, the meditation of which is devout exercise. Hence the reason for that command was none other than that the laws by which the king of Israel is obliged to rule his people, are set forth in Deuteronomy rather than in other books of the Old Testament, a fact

---

[15] *CIC, Digest*, I.I.I. This is also in Bracton, Woodbine edn, 24, from Azo, *Summa Instit.*, I.I., no.3.

[16] Romans 13:1.

[17] This is a reference to the thirteenth-century, pseudo-Aristotelian *Liber de Causis* (ed. O. Bardenhewer (Freiburg, 1882)). But Fortescue is likely to have used the popular *Auctoritates Aristotelis* for this reference, as he did for almost all of his citations of Aristotle. The *Auctoritates*, compiled possibly by Marsilius of Padua at Paris (See Hamesse edn), contains some 3000 citations, of varying accuracy, from the works of Aristotle (including the pseudo-Aristotelian *Liber de Causis* and *Secreta Secretorum*), together with extracts from the major commentaries of Averroës and Aquinas. It also contains some extracts from the works of Plato, Seneca and Boethius. The citation is from *Liber de Causis* I.14, 49–52 and is at *Auctoritates*, 231.

[18] II Chronicles 19:6.

which the circumstances of the command clearly show us.[19] Hence, Prince, the same reason impels you no less than the kings of Israel to be a careful student of the laws by which you will in future rule the people. For what is said to the king of Israel must be understood figuratively to apply to every king of a people acknowledging God.

Have I not, then, fitly and usefully proposed to you this command enjoined to the kings of Israel – to learn their law? For not only its example, but also, figuratively speaking, its authority, teach you and oblige you to act in the same way with regard to the laws of the kingdom which, by the permission of God, you are to inherit.'

Chapter IV
Here the Chancellor proves that the Prince can become happy and blessed through the laws

'The laws, most reverend Prince, not only invite you to fear God and thereby be wise, saying with the prophet, "Come children, hear me, and I will teach you the fear of the Lord",[20] but invite you also to their study, that you may obtain happiness and blessedness as far as they are obtainable in this life. For all the philosophers who have disputed so differently about happiness are agreed in this respect, namely, that happiness or blessedness is the end of all human desire. For that reason certain of them called it the *Summum Bonum*. The Peripatetics, however, placed it solely in virtue, the Stoics in what is honest, and the Epicureans in pleasure.[21] But since the Stoics defined honesty to be what is done well, laudably, and out of virtue, and the Epicureans asserted that nothing is pleasurable without virtue, all these schools, as Leonardus Aretinus says

---

[19] Fortescue here stresses that the analogy with Moses is not literal but figurative and is to be applied to the Prince's own particular circumstances, that is, it is to refer to the English law by which he shall rule his people. None of Fortescue's analogies (for example that of Rome, later) are to be applied literally and directly, but are rather to be adapted to the circumstances of the specific case under discussion.

[20] Psalms 34:11.

[21] The Peripatetics were followers of Aristotle (384–322BC), the Stoics were founded by Zeno of Citium (335–263BC) and the Epicureans followed the teachings of Epicurus (341–270BC), see J.H. Burns (ed.), *The Cambridge History of Medieval Political Thought c.350–c.1450*, ch.2.

in his *Isagogue of Moral Philosophy*, agreed in the view that virtue alone procures happiness.[22] Hence the Philosopher, in the seventh book of the *Politics*, in defining happiness, says that "It is the perfect exercise of virtues."[23]

These premises being granted, I want you to consider what follows from them. Human laws are none other than rules by which perfect justice is taught. But, to be sure, the justice which the laws disclose is not of the kind that is called commutative or distributive or any other particular virtue, but is itself the perfect virtue which is called by the name of legal justice and which the aforesaid Leonardus therefore says is perfect because it eliminates all vice and teaches every virtue, so that it is in itself justly called virtue.[24] Homer spoke of it in the same way as Aristotle in the fifth book of the *Ethics*, saying that "It is the most excellent of virtues, and neither Lucifer nor Hesperus is as wonderful as this."[25] This justice, indeed, is the object of all royal administration, because without it a king judges unjustly and is unable to fight rightfully. But this justice attained and truly observed, the whole office of a king is fairly discharged.

Therefore, since happiness is the perfect exercise of virtues, and human justice, which is not perfectly revealed except by the law, is not merely the effect of virtue, but is the whole virtue, it follows that he who enjoys justice is made happy by the law. Thereby he becomes blessed, for blessedness and happiness are the same in this fleeting life, and through justice he attains the *Summum Bonum* of this world. Not, indeed, that law can do this without grace, nor will you be able to learn further nor to strive after law or virtue, without grace. For, as Pariensis says in his book *Cur Deus Homo*, "The fundamental appetite of man for virtue is so vitiated by

---

[22] A copy of Leonardo Bruni's *Isagogue of Moral Philosophy* (*c*.1422) was given to the University of Oxford by Humphrey, duke of Gloucester in 1443. It is printed in H. Baron (ed.), *Leonardo Bruni Aretino Humanistisch-Philosophische Schriften* 20–41 and in English translation in G. Griffiths, J. Hankins and D. Thompson (eds.), *The Humanism of Leonardo Bruni*, 267–82. The section referred to by Fortescue is at Baron edn 27–8 and Griffiths *et al* edn. 273.

[23] *Auctoritates Aristotelis*, 261, from Aristotle, *Politics*, VII.viii.5.

[24] Bruni, *Isagogue of Moral Philosophy*, Baron edn 36 and Griffiths *et al* edn 279. This is a commentary on Aristotle, *Ethics*, v.

[25] *Auctoritates*, 238, from Aristotle, *Ethics*, v.i. 1129b27–30.

original sin, that to him the works of vice savour sweet and those of virtue bitter."[26] Wherefore that some give themselves to love and pursuit of virtues is a gift of the divine goodness, not derived from human merit. Are not, then, the laws which, guided and directed by grace, accomplish all these effects worthy to be studied with all application, since the learner of them shall obtain the happiness which according to the Philosopher is the end and completion of human desire, whereby he shall be blessed in this life, possessing its *Summum Bonum*?

Truly, if these considerations do not move you who are one day to rule the kingdom, the words of the prophet shall move you and oblige you to the study of the law, saying, "Be instructed, you who judge the earth."[27] For here the prophet does not persuade to a knowledge of any practical or mechanical art, for he does not say, "Be instructed, you who cultivate the earth", nor does he persuade to a knowledge of a wholly theoretical science, however suitable for the inhabitants of the earth, for he did not say in general terms, "Be instructed, you inhabitants of the earth." But the prophet invites kings only to the study of the law by which judgements are rendered, when he uses these specific words, "Be instructed, you who judge the earth". It follows on, "Lest at any time the Lord be angry, and you perish from the right way."[28] Nor, king's son, does holy scripture command you only to be instructed in the laws by which you shall pursue justice, but also, in another place, it requires you to love justice itself, when it says, "Love justice, you who judge the earth", Wisdom, chapter I.'[29]

Chapter V
Here he proves that ignorance of the law causes contempt for it

'But how shall you be able to love justice, if you do not first somehow grasp a knowledge of the laws by which justice itself is known?

---

[26] Pariensis is William of Auvergne, Bishop of Paris (d.1429). Fortescue had a copy of his *Cur Deus Homo* in his collection; an approximation to this quotation may be found at Bodleian Rawlinson MS C.398, fo.137v.
[27] Psalms 2:10.
[28] Psalms 2:12.
[29] Wisdom 1:1.

For Aristotle says that "Nothing is loved unless it is known."[30] Wherefore Fabius the Orator says that "The arts would be fortunate if artists alone were to judge them."[31] Indeed, what is not known is usually not only unloved but also spurned; hence a certain poet observes, "All that he is ignorant of, the rustic declares, ought to be despised."[32] And this view is that not only of the rustic, but also of learned experts. For, if a metaphysician tells a natural philosopher, who has never studied mathematics, that his science considers things disjoined from all matter and motion according to reality and reason; or a mathematician tells him that his science considers things conjoined with matter and motion according to reality but disjoined according to reason, the natural philosopher, who never knew anything disjoined from matter and motion in reality or reason,[33] rejects their sciences, though nobler than his own, and derides both of them, albeit they are philosophers, for no other reason than that he himself is utterly ignorant of their sciences.

Thus, you, Prince, would marvel at one learned in the laws of England if he told you that a brother shall not succeed in a paternal inheritance to a brother not born of the same mother, but that rather the inheritance shall descend to a sister of the whole blood or shall fall to the lord-in-chief of the fee as his escheat,[34] because you are ignorant of the reason for this law. But the difficulty of such a case does not in the least perturb one learned in the law of England. Wherefore it is commonly said that "Art has no enemy except the ignorant."[35] But far be it from you, king's son, to be hostile to or to despise the laws of the kingdom to which you are to succeed, when the book of Wisdom aforementioned instructs you to love the justice, which the laws reveal. Again and again, therefore, do I adjure you, most noble Prince, to learn the laws of your father's realm, to which you are to succeed, not only that you may avoid

---

[30] This is not to be found in *Auctoritates Aristotelis*. It is perhaps taken from another of Fortescue's sources, Augustine *On the Trinity*, x.ii.4.

[31] This has not been found in the works of Quintilian.

[32] Origin unknown.

[33] This is taken from Aquinas' commentary on Aristotle's *Metaphysics* VI, lect.1, n.1162 and is at *Auctoritates*, 127.

[34] For inheritance and the half-blood, see T.F.T. Plucknett, *A Concise History of the Common Law*, 719–22.

[35] Origin unknown.

those disadvantages, but because the human mind naturally desires the good and can desire nothing unless under expectation of good, and rejoices as soon as it has by instruction grasped the good, and loves it, and delights in it the more as it reflects upon it.

Hence you will realise that if by instruction you will understand those laws of which you are now ignorant, you will love them, since they are the best; and the more you investigate them, the more agreeably you will enjoy them. For all that is loved draws, by use, the lover of it into its own nature, wherefore, said Aristotle, "Use becomes another nature."[36] Thus, a sprig of a pear tree grafted on to an apple-stock, once it has taken, so draws the apple into the nature of a pear that both are deservedly called a pear tree, and produce the fruits of a pear. Thus, also, a virtue practised engenders a habit, so that the practiser thereof is thenceforth called by the name of the virtue.[37] Hence one practised in modesty is called modest, in continency, continent, in wisdom, wise. Wherefore, Prince, when you have done justice with pleasure, and have thereby become endued with the habit of law, you will deservedly be called just, and on that account it shall be said to you that "you have loved justice and hated iniquity, therefore the Lord thy God has anointed you with the oil of gladness above your fellows", that is to say, the kings of the earth.'[38]

Chapter VI
Here the Chancellor sums up the effect of his whole argument

'Are not these arguments, then, most serene Prince, enough to stir you to the study of the law? For you will thereby be endued with the habit of justice, and will therefore be called just; you will be able to avoid the disgrace of ignorance of the law, and, enjoying happiness through the law, you will be blessed in this life; you will moreover be imbued with the filial fear which is God's wisdom,

---

[36] The closest to Fortescue's 'Usus altera fit natura' is 'Consuetudo est altera natura' or 'Custom is another nature', from Aristotle, *Ethics* VII.x 1152a29–30, which is at *Auctoritates*, 241. It is also at *Auctoritates*, 272, taken from the *Secreta Secretorum*, xxiv.4.

[37] This is taken from Aristotle *Ethics*, II.i.

[38] Psalms 45:7.

and will, unperturbed, pursue the charity which is love towards God, thereby cleaving to God, as in the words of the Apostle, "You shall become one in spirit with Him."[39] But because this law cannot work in you without grace, it is necessary to pray for that above all things; also it is fitting for you to seek knowledge of the divine law and holy scripture. For holy writ says that "All are vain in whom subsists not the knowledge of God", Wisdom, chapter XIII.[40]

Therefore, Prince, whilst you are young and your mind is as it were a clean slate, impress on it these things, lest in future it be impressed more pleasurably with images of lesser worth;[41] for, as a certain wise man observes, "What a vessel takes when new it tastes of when it is old."[42] What craftsman is so negligent of his child's profit that he does not instruct him in crafts when he is young, by which he may afterwards gain the comforts of life? Thus a carpenter teaches his son to cut with an axe, the smith his son to work with a hammer, and he who desires to minister in spiritual matters is trained in letters. Thus it is proper for a prince to cause his son, who after him will rule the people, to be instructed in the laws whilst he is young. If the rulers of the earth would observe this, the world would be ruled with more justice than it now is. And if you do as I have urged you, you will offer no small example.'

Chapter VII
Now the Prince surrenders himself to the study of the laws, although he enquires further into certain precise points

The Chancellor having ceased, the Prince began thus, 'You have overcome me, good sir, with your most persuasive speech, by which you have made my mind burn with no small desire[43] for lessons in the law. Nevertheless, two things afflict my mind and puzzle me, just as a boat in troubled waters knows not wither to direct its bows.

---

[39] I Corinthians 6:17.
[40] Wisdom 13:1 (Vulgate).
[41] This may be a reference to Aristotle, *De Anima* III.4 (Penguin Classics, 1986) p.202, *Auctoritates*, 186, where the potential intellect is described as a *tabula rasa*.
[42] Origin unknown
[43] This is a rhetorical commonplace of this type of didactic dialogue, cf. Bruni, *Isagogue*, 22/269.

One is that when I recollect how many years students in the curricula of the law devote to their study before they attain to an adequate expertise therein, I fear lest I myself spend the years of my youth in the same way.[44] The second is whether I shall devote myself to the study of the laws of England or of the civil laws which are renowned throughout the world. For the people should not be ruled by any save the best laws; as Aristotle says, "Nature always covets the best."[45] Hence I should willingly pay heed to your advice in these things.'

Chapter VIII
As much knowledge of the law as is necessary for a prince is speedily attainable

To whom the Chancellor replied, 'These matters, king's son, are not so hidden in mystery that they need lengthy deliberation, so I will not delay in telling you how I see them. Aristotle, in the first book of the *Physics*, says that "We think we know anything when we know the causes and principles of it as far as its elements."[46] On this the Commentator observes that "Aristotle meant by principles, effective causes, and by causes, final causes, and by elements, matter and form."[47] In the laws, indeed, there is no matter and form as in natural things and in artificial compounds. But, nevertheless, there are in them certain elements out of which they proceed as out of matter and form, such as customs, statutes, and the law of nature, from which all the laws of the realm proceed as natural things do out of matter and form, just as all we read comes out of the letters which are also called elements.

The principles, furthermore, which the Commentator said are effective causes, are certain universals which those learned in the

---

[44] In ch.L, Fortescue states that it is necessary to study for at least sixteen years to become a serjeant-at-law, below 72. In ch.VIII, he says it takes twenty years to become a judge, (below 16).

[45] Fortescue's citation is a combination of Aristotle, *Ethics*, I.xiii 1102b14, *Auctoritates*, 234, which has 'reason' instead of 'nature' and Aristotle, *On generation and corruption*, II 536b27–28, *Auctoritates*, 170 which states 'nature always desires that which is the better'.

[46] *Auctoritates*, 140, from Aristotle, *Physics*, I.1 184a12–14.

[47] 'The Commentator' is Averroës (1126–1198) and the statement is at *Auctoritates*, 143.

laws of England and mathematicians alike call maxims, just as rhetoricians speak of paradoxes, and civilians of principles of law.[48] These principles, indeed, are not discerned by force of argument nor by logical demonstrations, but they are arrived at, as it is taught in the second book of the *Posteriora*, by induction through the senses and the memory.[49] Wherefore, Aristotle says in the first book of the *Physics* that "Principles do not proceed out of other things nor out of one another, but other things proceed out of them."[50] Hence in the first book of the *Topica* it is written that "Any principle is its own ground for holding it."[51] For that reason, Aristotle says, "There is no arguing with those who deny principles",[52] because, as it is written in the sixth book of *Ethics*, "There is no rational ground for principles."[53] Therefore, whoever is anxious to understand any branch of knowledge must learn thoroughly its principles. For out of them are discovered the final causes to which one is brought by process of reasoning upon a knowledge of principles.

Hence if these three, that is, principles, causes, and elements are unknown, the science to which they appertain is totally unknown; and if these are known the science is known, not indeed precisely, but at any rate generally and as a whole. Thus we declare we know the divine law when we feel we know faith, charity, hope, as well as the sacraments of the church, and the commandments of God, leaving other mysteries of theology to the prelates of the church. Wherefore the Lord said to His disciples, "Unto you it is given to know the mystery of the kingdom of God, but to others in parables, that seeing they may not see."[54] And the Apostle said, "Know not more than you ought to know",[55] and in another place, "Knowing not high things".[56]

---

[48] The 'regulae iuris' or 'principles of law' consist of over 200 short fragments of civil law, collected together in *CIC, Digest*, 50.17, entitled 'De diversis regulis iuris antiqui'. For their use and significance, see P.G. Stein, *Regulae Iuris*.
[49] *Auctoritates*, 321, from Aristotle, *Posterior Analytics* II 100b3–5.
[50] *Auctoritates*, 141, from Aristotle, *Physics* I.v 188a28–29.
[51] *Auctoritates*, 321, from Aristotle, *Topics* I 100b19–21.
[52] *Auctoritates*, 140, from Aristotle, *Physics* I.ii 185a1–2.
[53] *Auctoritates*, 241, from Aristotle, *Ethics* VI.viii 1142a25–26.
[54] Mark 4:11–12.
[55] Romans 12:3.
[56] Romans 12:16.

Thus you, Prince, do not need to explore the mysteries of the law of England by long study; it is sufficient for you to progress in the laws as you have in grammar. Perfection, indeed, in grammar, which flows out of etymology, orthography, prosody, and syntax, as out of four streams, you have not completely acquired, yet you are sufficiently learned in grammar to be deservedly called a grammarian. Similarly, you will deserve to be called a lawyer if you have learned, in the manner of a student, the principles and causes of the law as far as the elements.

For it will not be expedient for you to search out the sacred mysteries of the law by the exertion of your own reason, these should rather be left to your judges and advocates who in the kingdom of England are called serjeants-at-law,[57] and also to others skilled in the law who are commonly called apprentices.[58] In fact, you will render judgements better through others than by yourself, for none of the kings of England is seen to give judgement by his own lips, yet all the judgements of the realm are his, though given through others, just as Jehoshaphat asserted that "All judicial sentences are the judgements of God."[59] Wherefore, most gracious Prince, you will be sufficiently learned in the laws of the kingdom in a short time and with moderate industry, provided you devote your mind to the apprehension of them. For Seneca said, in a letter to Lucilius, "There is nothing which great pains and diligent care do not overcome."[60] Indeed I know the perspicacity of your mind, and I dare say that in these laws, though the experience of them necessary for judges is scarcely attainable in the labours of twenty years, you will adequately acquire a knowledge fitting for a prince in one year. But in the meantime, do not neglect the military exercises to which you are ardently devoted, but enjoy them at pleasure as a recreation even during that year.'

---

[57] Cf. 'it is enough for a subject that he acknowledges the commands of the law, as for a servant the will of his lord, while the higher mysteries of the law remain for those learned in the law', *On the Nature of the Law of Nature*, I.xlvi. It is clear that the king, like his subjects, is *sub lege*. On the serjeants-at-law and their high status, see ch.L, below 70–3.

[58] On apprentices-at-law, see Plucknett, *Concise History*, 217–19.

[59] II Chronicles 19:6.

[60] Seneca, *Letter to Lucilius* in *Auctoritates*, 276.

Chapter IX
A king ruling politically is not able to change the laws of the kingdom

'The second point, Prince, about which you are apprehensive, shall be removed with like ease. For you doubt whether you should apply yourself to the study of the laws of the English or of the civil laws, because the civil laws are celebrated with a glorious fame throughout the world above all other human laws. Do not, king's son, let this consideration trouble you.[61] For the king of England is not able to change the laws of his kingdom at pleasure, for he rules his people with a government not only royal but also political. If he were to rule over them with a power only royal, he would be able to change the laws of the realm, and also impose on them tallages and other burdens without consulting them; this is the sort of dominion which the civil laws indicate when they state that "What pleased the prince has the force of law."[62] But it is far otherwise with the king ruling his people politically, because he himself is not able to change the laws without the assent of his subjects nor to burden an unwilling people with strange impositions, so that, ruled by laws that they themselves desire, they freely enjoy their goods, and are despoiled neither by their own king nor any other. The people rejoice in the same way under a king ruling only royally, provided he does not degenerate into a tyrant. Of such a king, the Philosopher said in the third book of the *Politics* that "It is better for a city to be ruled by the best man than by the best law."[63]

But, because it does not always happen that the man presiding over a people is of this sort, St Thomas, in the book he wrote for the king of Cyprus, *On Princely Government*, is considered to have desired that a kingdom be constituted such that the king may not

---

[61] The 'choice' which the Chancellor puts to the Prince is a matter of the Prince's deciding or choosing to learn, live and rule by the laws of England. Having made that decision, he shall have properly orientated his will, that is, he shall be right-willing and shall therefore see that his power is not such that he can change the laws, and that to desire to do so would be to prefer private to public good, that is, to become a tyrant.

[62] This is the *lex regia* and is found in several places in the *Corpus Iuris Civilis*, including *Institutes*, I, 2, 6 and *Digest* I, 4, 1.

[63] *Auctoritates*, 256, from Peter of Auvergne's commentary *On the Politics*, III, lect.14, n.490.

be free to govern his people tyrannically, which only comes to pass when the royal power is restrained by political law. Rejoice, therefore, good Prince, that such is the law of the kingdom to which you are to succeed, because it will provide no small security and comfort for you and for the people. By such a law, as the aforementioned Saint said, "the whole human race would have been ruled, if it had not transgressed the commands of God in paradise."[64] By such a law the synagogue was ruled under God alone as king, who adopted it as a realm peculiarly His, and defended it; but at last, a human king having been constituted for it, on its own petition, it was successively humiliated by only royal laws. Under these, none the less, it rejoiced when the best kings ruled, but when an undisciplined sort ruled, it lamented inconsolably, as the Books of Kings reveal more clearly.[65] But as I think I have discussed this matter sufficiently in a small work *Of the Nature of the Law of Nature*[66] which I wrote for your consideration, I desist from saying more about it now.'

Chapter X
A question by the Prince

Then the Prince said, 'How does it come to be, Chancellor, that one king is able to rule his people only royally, and the same power is denied to the other king? Of equal rank, since both are kings, I cannot help wondering why they are unequal in power.'

Chapter XI
A reference to the other treatise

Chancellor: 'It is sufficiently shown, in the small work I have mentioned, that the king ruling politically is of no less power than he who rules his people royally, as he wishes;[67] but I have by no means denied, either then or now, that their authority over their subjects

---

[64] Thomas Aquinas, *On Princely Government*, i.vi.
[65] This refers to the four Books of Kings which are I and II Samuel and I and II Kings.
[66] *On the Nature of the Law of Nature*, i.xvi, see Appendix A, below, 127.
[67] *On the Nature of the Law of Nature*, i.xxvi, see Appendix A, below 133.

is different. The cause of this diversity I will explain to you as far as I can.'

Chapter XII
How kingdoms ruled only royally first began

'Formerly, men excelling in power, greedy of dignity and glory, subjugated neighbouring peoples to themselves, often by force, and compelled them to serve them, and to submit to their commands, to which in time they themselves gave sanction as laws for those people. The people thus subject, by long endurance, and as long as they were protected by their subjection against the injuries of others, consented to the dominion of their subduers, thinking it better to be under the government of one, whereby they were protected from others, than to be exposed to the oppressions of all those who wished to attack them. And thus began certain kingdoms, and the subduers of them ruling the subject people in this way, usurped to themselves the name of king, from the word "ruling",[68] and their dominion is described as only royal.

So Nimrod first procured for himself a kingdom, though he was not himself a king, but is called by holy scripture a mighty hunter before the Lord,[69] because, as a hunter compels beasts enjoying their liberty to obey him, so did he compel men. Thus Belus reduced the Assyrians to his behest, and Ninus the greater part of Asia.[70] Thus the Romans usurped the government of the world, and likewise kingdoms began among nearly all peoples. Hence, when the children of Israel demanded a king as all people then had, the Lord was thereby displeased, and commanded the royal law to be explained to them by a prophet – the law which was none other than the pleasure of the king ruling over them, as may be learned more fully in the

---

[68] The derivation 'rex a regendo' is found in Augustine, *City of God* v.12 and in several places in Isidore of Seville's *Etymologies*, including vII.xii and Ix.3, see J. Balogh, 'Rex a recte regendo', *Speculum* III (1928), 580–2. Bracton also uses it: 'for he is called *rex* not from reigning, but from ruling well, since he is a king as long as he rules well, but a tyrant when he oppresses by violent domination the people entrusted to his care', *Laws and Customs*, Woodbine edn, 305.

[69] Genesis 10:9.

[70] Augustine, *City of God*, xvi.17. Cf. *On the Nature of the Law of Nature*, I.vIII and II.xLVI.

first book of Kings.[71] Now you have, most excellent Prince, unless I am mistaken, the form of the beginning of kingdoms possessed royally. I shall now, therefore, also try to explain how the kingdom ruled politically first began, so that, the beginnings of both kingdoms being known, the reason for the diversity about which you enquire may be more easily made plain to you.'

Chapter XIII
How kingdoms ruled politically first began

'Saint Augustine, in the nineteenth book of *The City of God*, chapter 23, said that "A people is a group of men united by consent of law and by community of interest."[72] But such a people does not deserve to be called a body whilst it is acephalous, that is, without a head. Because, just as in natural things, what is left over after decapitation is not a body, but what we call a trunk, so in political things, a community without a head is not by any means a body. Hence Aristotle in the first book of the *Politics* said that "Whensoever one body is constituted out of many, one will rule, and the others be ruled."[73]

So a people that wills to erect itself into a kingdom or any other body politic must always set up one man for the government of all that body, who, by analogy with a kingdom, is, from "ruling", usually called a king.[74] Just as in this way the physical body grows out of the embryo, regulated by one head, so the kingdom issues from the people, and exists as a body mystical, governed by one man as head. And just as in the body natural, as the Philosopher said, the heart is the first living thing,[75] having in itself the blood which it sends forth to all the members, whereby they are quickened and

---

[71] I. Samuel 8.

[72] This is Augustine, *City of God*, XIX.21, where Augustine is citing Scipio's definition of a commonwealth or *respublica*, taken from Cicero, *De Re Publica* I.xxv.39.

[73] *Auctoritates*, 252, from Aristotle, *Politics*, I.v.3.

[74] For 'rex a regendo', see above n. 68.

[75] Aristotle, *On the Parts of Animals* II.iv: 'In embryos, as soon as they are formed, the heart can be seen moving before any of the other parts.' There is something similar at *Auctoritates*, 218–219, but Fortescue is closer to the original.

live,[76] so in the body politic the intention of the people[77] is the first living thing, having in it the blood, namely, political provision[78] for the interest of the people, which it transmits to the head and all the members of the body, by which the body is nourished and quickened.

The law, indeed, by which a group of men is made into a people, resembles the sinews of the physical body, for, just as the body is held together by the sinews, so this body mystical is bound together and preserved as one by the law, which is derived from the word "binding",[79] and the members and bones of this body, which signify the solid basis of truth by which the community is sustained, preserve their rights through the law, as the body natural does through the sinews. And just as the head of the physical body is unable to change its sinews, or to deny its members proper strength and due nourishment of blood, so a king who is head of the body politic is unable to change the laws of that body, or to deprive that same people of their own substance uninvited or against their wills.

You have here, Prince, the form of the institution of the political kingdom, whence you can estimate the power that the king can exercise in respect of the law and the subjects of such a realm; for

---

[76] Aristotle, *On the Parts of Animals*, II.iv: 'The heart is itself the source and spring of the blood', 'the blood is the matter of which the whole body consists – matter in the case of living creatures being nourishment'. Fortescue is closer to the original than to *Auctoritates*, 219.

[77] I have altered the translation of 'intencio' from 'will' to 'intention', because there is a significant difference between intention and will in scholastic analyses of human action. The intention of the people is realised in action by the will of the prince, only after deliberation and consent, see my Introduction, above xxvii–xxix.

[78] I have altered the translation of 'provisionem politicam' from 'political forethought' to 'political provision' in order to maintain the semantic link with 'providere', which is in turn associated with 'prudence', the political virtue needed in order to deliberate successfully about the means to a future goal, see my Introduction, above xxvii–xxix.

[79] Cf. 'the law of custom (*lex consuetudinis*) ... and the law of nature (*lex naturae*) ... are not named from *legendo* (reading), but from *ligando* (binding) because they bind and are not always read ... whence law may be called the bond of right (*iuris vinculum*), by which a man is constrained to do or suffer what is just (*iustum*)', *On the Nature of the Law of Nature* I.XXX. The derivation 'lex a ligando' is from Alexander of Hales (*c.* 1185–1245), *Summa Universae Theologiae*, IV.III.2 *inq.* 1 *quaest, unica*, n.224, ed. Quarracchi (1948), 315. The derivation 'lex a legendo' that Fortescue dismisses is from Isidore of Seville's *Etymologies*, V.iii.2.

a king of this sort is set up for the protection[80] of the law, the subjects, and their bodies and goods, and he has power to this end issuing from the people, so that it is not permissible for him to rule his people with any other power. In this way I briefly answer the question you desire to be assured of – the question of how it came to be that the power of kings should differ so widely. I am firmly of the opinion that this difference is due solely to diversity in the institution of those dignities which I have mentioned, as you can understand by the light of reason from what has been said.

For thus the kingdom of England blossomed forth into a political and royal dominion out of Brutus' band of Trojans, whom he led out of the territories of Italy and of the Greeks.[81] And thus Scotland, which was obedient thereto as a duchy, grew into a political and royal kingdom.[82] Many other realms also have been destined by such an origin as this to be ruled not only royally, but also politically. Hence Diodorus Siculus, in the second book of the *Ancient Histories*, writes thus of the Egyptians: "The kings of Egypt did not at first lead their lives with licence as other rulers, to whom will is law, but, like private people, they were restrained by the laws; nor were they thereby displeased, but thought themselves fortunate in obeying the laws; for they considered those who indulged their own cupidities did much which exposed them to dangers and perils."[83] And in the fourth book he writes thus: "He who became king of Ethiopia led a life ruled by laws, and did everything according to the custom of the country, offering neither reward nor penalty to anyone except according to the law handed down to him

---

[80] The phrase here is 'ad tutelam . . . (e)rectus est'; the king ruling politically is like a tutor or guardian to the people entrusted to his care. This Roman law notion of tutelage combines with the concept of kingship as a ministry in which the king administers justice to the people, as a shepherd to God's flock, see for example Ezekiel 34, used extensively by Aquinas in Book I of *On Princely Government* and by his continuator Ptolemy of Lucca.

[81] The Brutus legend is contained most famously in Geoffrey of Monmouth, *History of the Kings of Britain*, I.16–18, but the story also occurs in two works in Fortescue's possession – Rede's chronicle and Vincent of Beauvais.

[82] Scotland was never obedient to England as a duchy. Its designation as a political and royal kingdom must be due to the combination of monarchy and parliament, although parliamentary consent was not needed in Scotland for legislation or taxation.

[83] Diodorus Siculus, *Library of History*, II.35. The first five books of this work were translated by Poggio Bracciolini (1380–1459), and it is this translation that Fortescue cites.

from his predecessors." The same is said of the king of Saba in happy Arabia and of other kings who reigned happily in ancient times.'[84]

Chapter XIV
Here the Prince briefly sums up what the Chancellor has previously declared more fully

The Prince replies, 'You have, Chancellor, by the light of your declaration, dispelled the darkness that dulled the acuity of my mind, so that I now very clearly perceive that no people ever incorporated themselves into a kingdom by their own agreement and will,[85] unless in order to possess safer than before both themselves and their own, which they feared to lose – a design which would be thwarted if their king were able to deprive them of their means, which was not permitted before to anyone among men. And such a people would suffer still more grievously if they were ruled by laws strange, and perhaps hateful, to them; especially if their substance was thereby diminished; to avoid the loss of which, as well as to protect their bodies, they submitted of their own will to the government of a king. Truly such a power as this could not issue from the people, and if not from them, a king of this sort could obtain no power over them.

On the other hand, I conceive it to be quite otherwise with a kingdom which is incorporated solely by the authority and power of the king, because such a people is subjected to him by no sort of agreement other than to obey and be ruled by his laws, which are the pleasure of him by the pleasure of whose will the people is made into a realm. Nor, Chancellor, has it thus far slipped my memory that you have shown elsewhere, with learned argument, in your treatise *Of the Nature of the Law of Nature*, that the power of the two kings is equal,[86] since the power by which one of them is free to do wrong does not increase his freedom, just as to be able

---

[84] *Ibid.*, IV, 76.

[85] Note that the realm self-incorporates 'all-in-one-go'; the people agrees to become a body politic and that body 'grows' a head as if by nature. In *The Governance* there is a more explicit distinction between the act of will that incorporates the people and the act of will that 'chooses' the king, see *Governance*, ch. 2, below 86.

[86] *On the Nature of the Law of Nature*, I.xxvi, see Appendix A, 133–6.

to be ill or to die is not power, but is rather to be deemed impotency because of the deprivation involved. For, as Boethius said, "There is no power unless for good",[87] so that to be able to do evil, as the king reigning royally can more freely do than the king ruling his people politically, diminishes rather than increases his power. For the holy spirits who, already confirmed in glory, are unable to sin, are more powerful than we, who with a free rein take delight in any deed.[88]

Therefore, it only remains for me to enquire of you whether the law of England, to the study of which you urge me, is as good and effectual for the government of that kingdom as the civil law, by which the Holy Empire is ruled, is thought to be sufficient for the government of the whole world.[89] If you satisfy me in this respect, with suitable proof, I shall at once apply myself to the study of the law, and shall not weary you any more with my queries in these matters.'

Chapter XV
All laws are the law of nature, customs, or statutes

Chancellor: 'You have committed to memory, my good Prince, what I have so far mentioned to you, so that you deserve my explanation of what you now ask. I want you, then, to know that all human laws are either law of nature, customs, or statutes, which are also called constitutions. But customs and the judgements of the law of nature, after they have been reduced to writing, and promulgated by the sufficient authority of the prince, and commanded to be kept, are changed into a constitution or something of the nature of statutes. Thereupon they oblige the prince's subjects to keep them

---

[87] Boethius, *Consolation of Philosophy*, IV.ii.24. The sense of this is at *Auctoritates*, 291, but, as is clear from his references to it in *On the Nature of the Law of Nature*, Fortescue knew more of this work than the extracts contained in *Auctoritates*.

[88] This idea of 'non-powers' or 'impotency' is very important to Fortescue's argument, since it is his main defence against claims that the king ruling politically must therefore have limited power. His argument is that the king is raised to a higher, more divine nature, in that, like the angels and God, he is unable to sin, and, like them, is thereby more powerful and more free. Cf. *Governance*, chs. 6 and 19, 95 and 122, and *On the Nature of the Law of Nature*, I.xxvi, Appendix A, 133.

[89] See Justinian's own claims for his body of law in 'Deo auctore', in P. Kreuger, T. Mommsen and A. Watson (eds.) *The Digest of Justinian*.

under greater penalty than before, by reason of the strictness of that command. Such is no small part of the civil law, which is reduced to writing by the Roman princes in large volumes, and by their authority commanded to be observed.[90] Hence that part has now obtained the name of civil law, like the other statutes of the emperors.

If, therefore, I shall prove that the law of England excels preeminently in respect of these three fountains, so to speak, of all law, I shall have proven also that law to be good and effectual for the government of the realm.[91] Furthermore, if I shall have clearly shown it to be adapted to the utility of that same realm as the civil law is to the good of the Empire, I shall have made manifest that the law is not only excellent, but also, like the civil law, is the best choice, which is what you desire.[92] Therefore, I proceed to show you sufficiently these two things.'

Chapter XVI
The law of nature is the same in all regions

'The laws of England, in those points which they sanction by reason of the law of nature, are neither better nor worse in their

---

[90] This is a reference to the *Corpus Iuris Civilis* which was declared to be and to have the authority of written law or 'lex' by Justinian, see P.G. Stein, 'Roman Law', in Burns (ed.), *Cambridge History of Medieval Political Thought*, ch. 3, esp. 42–7.

[91] In *On the Nature of the Law of Nature*, I.xliii, Fortescue states that 'the laws of man shine and differ like the stars', every planet having 'its proper functions within its proper sphere, wherein it develops the power of its own nature'. The Chancellor seeks to demonstrate firstly that the laws of England are 'good and effective' for the realm of England, just as the civil laws are good for the Empire, each in their own proper sphere. Only then, does he go on to show their absolute superiority with respect to truth and justice.

[92] The Chancellor seeks to prove that the laws of the realm of England are 'excellent', 'most desirable' and 'most eligible or worthy to be chosen'. This is a matter of bringing the Prince to see that he must know the laws because it is through them that he shall be able to imprint the virtue of justice on his mind so that he is habituated to virtue and becomes just, having thereby that constant and perpetual will to justice which is essential to his future office. Cf. 'that power of the human soul which is called will, and oftentimes wills good and often evil, is not always justice, which is virtue. But whenever the said will firmly wills justice, then by reason of its union with justice, the whole will has the name of justice and may be called steadfast and perpetual', *On the Nature of the Law of Nature*, I.xl. The Prince must choose to embrace the laws.

judgements than are all laws of other nations in like cases. For, as Aristotle said, in the fifth book of the *Ethics*, "Natural law is that which has the same force among all men."[93] Wherefore there is no need to discuss it further. But from now on we must examine what are the customs, and also the statutes, of England, and we shall first look at the characteristics of those customs.'

Chapter XVII
The customs of England are very ancient, and have been used and accepted by five nations successively

'The kingdom of England was first inhabited by Britons, then ruled by Romans, then again by Britons and then it was possessed by Saxons, who changed its name from Britain to England. Then for a short time the kingdom was dominated by Danes, and then again by Saxons, but finally by Normans, whose posterity hold the realm at the present time. And throughout the period of these nations and their kings, the realm has been continuously regulated by the same customs as it is now,[94] customs which, if they had not been the best, some of those kings would have changed for the sake of justice or by the impulse of caprice, and totally abolished them, especially the Romans, who judged almost the whole of the rest of the world by their laws. Similarly, others of these aforesaid kings, who possessed the kingdom of England only by the sword, could, by that power, have destroyed its laws.[95] Indeed, neither the civil laws of the Romans, so deeply rooted by the usage of so many ages, nor the laws of the Venetians, which are renowned above others for their antiquity – though their island was uninhabited, and Rome unbuilt at the time of the origin of the Britons – nor the laws of

---

[93] *Auctoritates*, 239, from Aristotle, *Ethics*, v.vii 1134b19–21.

[94] English customs have always been the same because they have always been the customs of the English people, that is, they have always been the usages of the English people. Cf. 'quod plures vel omnes eligunt, magis est eligendum', *Auctoritates* 324, from Aristotle, *Topics* III 116a13–14 and 'mutatio consuetudinis non est subita, sed successiva', *Auctoritates* 272, from pseudo-Aristotle *Secreta Secretorum* XXXIV.4.

[95] Fortescue does not deny the existence of the Norman Conquest, merely its effect, because to admit of a fundamental change in the constitution brought about by the force of conquest would be to state that the king of England now ruled 'only royally' by his own laws. For the consequences of Norman rule for the study of English law, see ch.XLVIII, below 66.

any Christian kingdom, are so rooted in antiquity. Hence there is no gainsaying nor legitimate doubt but that the customs of the English are not only good but the best.'[96]

Chapter XVIII
Here he shows with what solemnity statutes are promulgated in England

'It only remains, then, to examine whether or not the statutes of the English are good. These, indeed, do not emanate from the will of the prince alone, as do the laws in kingdoms which are governed only royally, where so often statutes secure the advantage of their maker only, thereby redounding to the loss and undoing of the subjects. Sometimes, also, by the negligence of such princes and the inertia of their counsellors, those statutes are promulgated so ill-advisedly that they deserve the name of corruptions rather than of laws. But the statutes of England cannot so arise, since they are made not only by the prince's will, but also by the assent of the whole realm, so they cannot be injurious to the people nor fail to secure their advantage.[97] Furthermore, it must be supposed that they are necessarily replete with prudence and wisdom, since they are promulgated by the prudence not of one counsellor nor of a hundred only, but of more than three hundred chosen men[98] – of

---

[96] This is not a claim that the laws are best *because* they are most ancient. Fortescue states that English laws are best because they are most just and have therefore not had to be changed. Thus the antiquity of the laws is the proof that they are the best, not the reason for their being so.

[97] This is the idea that no-one willingly harms themself which was a feature of medieval corporation theory, see J.P. Canning, 'Law, Sovereignty and Corporation Theory 1300–1450' in Burns (ed.), *Cambridge History of Medieval Political Thought*, 454–76.

[98] H.L. Gray's work, *The Influence of the Commons on Early Legislation* (Cambridge, Mass., 1932) showed that most of the statutes between 1399 and 1450 derived from Commons bills as opposed to official bills and that, from 1429, the style 'a ceste bille les communes sont assentuz' was used, 414. Also in 1429 the franchise was limited to forty shilling freeholders and the majority principle was recognised in the election of knights and burgesses, see J.S. Roskell, *The Commons in the Parliament of 1422: English Society and Parliamentary Legislation under the Lancastrians* (Manchester, 1954), 13–14. See also J.G. Edwards, 'The *Plena Potestas* of English Parliamentary Representatives' in *Oxford Essays in Medieval History*, 141–54 and A.L. Brown, *The Governance of Late Medieval England 1272–1461* (London, 1989), chs. 8–10.

such a number as once the Senate of the Romans was once ruled by[99] – as those who know the form of the summons, the order, and the procedure of parliament can more clearly describe.[100] And if statutes ordained with such solemnity and care happen not to give full effect to the intention of the makers, they can speedily be revised, and yet not without the assent of the commons and nobles of the realm, in the manner in which they first originated.[101] Thus, Prince, all the kinds of the law of England are now plain to you. You will be able to estimate their merits by your own prudence, and by comparison with other laws; and when you find none in the world so excellent, you will be bound to confess that they are not only good, but the most desirable to you.'

Chapter XIX
Here he lays down the manner in which the character of the civil and the English laws can be discerned

'Only one point of those that puzzled you now remains to be explained, namely, whether the laws of England deserve to be

---

[99] The number of Roman senators was traditionally said to be 300, see H.F. Jolow-icz, *A Historical Introduction to the Study of Roman Law* (Cambridge, 1952), 27–43, esp. 28.

[100] Fortescue had himself sat in parliament eight times (Chrimes, *De laudibus*, lix-lxvii) and he is perhaps here referring to the *Modus Tenendi Parlamentum* (*c.*1324), a copy of which he had in his collection (Bodleian Rawlinson MS C398). The *Modus* stressed the representative and political nature of parliament, see N. Pronay and J. Taylor (eds.), *Parliamentary Texts of the later Middle Ages* (Oxford, 1980), 67–114.

[101] Fortescue's understanding of law as 'made' is one of the most significant aspects of his theory. Statute law is seen as a positive feature of government which facili-tates reform and progress towards better government. It is law made by the assent of the whole realm in the institution which is representative of the whole realm. Cf. Bracton: 'it will not be absurd to call English laws *leges*, though they are unwritten, since whatever has been rightly decided and approved with the counsel and consent of the magnates and the general agreement of the *res publica*, the authority of the king or prince having first been added thereto, has the force of law, since they [English laws] have been approved by the consent of those who use them, and confirmed by the oath of kings, they cannot be nullified without their consent, but may be changed for the better, for to change for the better is not to nullify. If new and unusual matters arise which have not before been seen in the realm . . . let them be adjourned to the great court to be there determined by counsel of the court', *On the Laws and Customs of England*, 21. Fortescue's contemporary Reginald Pecock (*c.*1395-*c.*1460) wrote that 'it is lawful for princes

adjudged as fitting, effective, and convenient for this kingdom of England as the civil laws are for the Empire. Comparisons, indeed, Prince, as I remember you said at one time, are reputed odious, and so I am not fond of making them but you will be able to gather more effectively whether both of these laws are of equal merit, or whether one more richly deserves praise than the other, not from my opinion, but from those points wherein their judgements differ. For where both laws agree, they are equally praiseworthy, but in the cases wherein they differ, the superiorities of the more excellent law will appear after due reflection.[102] Let us, therefore, bring forward some cases of this sort, so that you can weigh in a fair balance which of the laws shows its superiorities better and more justly. And first let us propound the most important of such cases.'

Chapter XX
The first case in which the civil and the English laws differ

'If parties before a judge come to joinder of issue on the matters of fact, which those learned in the laws of England call "the issue of the plea", the truth of such issue ought, by the civil laws, to be proved by the deposition of witnesses, for which two suitable witnesses suffice.[103] But by the laws of England, the truth cannot be settled for the judge, unless by the oath of twelve men of the neighbourhood where the fact is supposed to have been located.[104] The question, therefore, is which of those two very different procedures

---

with their commonalty to make politic and civil laws and ordinances for the better rule of the people in temporal and civil government', *Repressor*, II, 454, cited in N. Doe, *Fundamental Authority in late medieval English Law*, 13 n31. See also Doe, 'Fifteenth-century concepts of law', 270–5.

[102] In the following comparisons Fortescue presents a deliberately idealised picture of the form and procedure of the common law system, in order to highlight the gap between ideal and reality: having stated that there is a mechanism for reform, he now shows the extent to which it is needed.

[103] On civil law witness procedure, see W.W. Buckland, *A Textbook of Roman Law from Augustus to Justinian* ed. P.G. Stein (3rd edn, Cambridge, 1975), 632–7 and 662 and A. Esmein, *A History of Continental Criminal Procedure with special reference to France* (London, 1914).

[104] On the English system of trial by jury, see Plucknett, *Concise History*, ch.4 and J.S. Cockburn and T.A. Green (eds), *Twelve Good Men and True: The Criminal Trial Jury in England 1200–1800* (Princeton, 1988), esp.ch.4.

should be held to be more reasonable and effective for the discovery of the truth thus in doubt. For the law that can reveal it better and more certainly is superior in this respect to the law that is of less effect and virtue. Hence let us proceed thus in the examination of this matter.'

Chapter XXI
Here are described the evils that come of a law which admits proof only by witnesses

'By the civil law, the party who has taken the affirmative in the joinder of issue ought to produce the witnesses, whom he shall name at his pleasure. But a negative cannot be proven, at least not directly, though it may be indirectly. He who cannot find, out of all the men he knows, two who are so lacking in conscience and truth that, for fear, love, or advantage, they will contradict every truth, is deemed feeble indeed and of little diligence. These, then, the party can produce as witnesses in his cause. And if the other party wants to object to them or to their evidence, it does not always happen that they, their conduct, and their habits are known to he who wishes to object, so that such witnesses could be rejected on account of their depravity and viciousness. And since their statements are in the affirmative, they are not easily disproved by circumstantial or other indirect evidence.

Who, then, can live secure of himself or his own under such a law – a law that offers assistance to anyone hostile to him? And what two rogues are so heedless that they do not, before they are produced as witnesses, privately frame a likely story and account of the fact about which they are to be examined in court, and piece together all the details as they would have been if the story were true? "For the children of this world", said the Lord, "are more prudent than the children of light."[105]

Thus the most wicked Jezebel brought forth two witnesses, sons of Belial, against Naboth in proceedings by which he lost his life, and Ahab his king took possession of his vineyard.[106] So Susanna, a most chaste wife, would have been put to death for adultery by

---

[105] Luke 16:8.
[106] I Kings 21: 5–16.

the testimony of two old men, themselves judges, if the Lord had not miraculously freed her by means of an inconceivable prudence which of nature the youth did not have, being not yet advanced in years.[107] And if that same boy Daniel proved them false because of the variance in their depositions, who but the Lord alone could have known that they would differ so in their statements, since there was no legal obligation for them to remember under what kind of tree the alleged deed was done? For the witnesses of a crime are not supposed to notice every bush and other circumstance concerning the fact, if they have very little effect in aggravating or detecting the crime. But when those judges differed as to the species of the tree, their depositions were good for nothing, and their own words showed that they had been prevaricators of the truth, so that they deservedly incurred the penalty they had intended for the accused.

You know well, most gracious Prince, that recently master John Fringe, after he had been active in priest's orders for three years, was compelled to relinquish his holy orders and to consummate a marriage with a young woman to whom, according to the deposition of two rogues, he had previously been betrothed. Being convicted of the crime of conspiracy of treason against your highness, after having lived with her for fourteen years and having raised seven children, he confessed, at the moment of his death and in front of all the people, that those witnesses had been suborned and had given false testimony.[108] The perversion of judgements by false witness in this way, even under the best judges, is no news to you, nor is it unknown in the world, for this crime is, alas!, very often committed.'

Chapter XXII
See here the inhumanity of tortures

'The law of France, therefore, is not content to convict the accused in capital cases by witnesses, lest innocent blood be condemned by the testimony of liars. But that law prefers the accused to be racked

---

[107] Daniel 13 (Vulgate).
[108] The information on the case of John Fringe is discussed in Chrimes, *De laudibus*, 163–5.

with tortures until they themselves confess to their guilt,[109] than to proceed by the deposition of witnesses who are often provoked to perjury by wicked passions and sometimes by the subornation of evil persons. By such craft and cunning, criminals and suspected criminals are afflicted with so many kinds of tortures in that kingdom that the pen shrinks from putting them into writing.[110]

Some are stretched on racks, whereby their sinews are lacerated and their veins gush out streams of blood. The tendons and joints of some are sundered by divers suspended weights.[111] The mouths of others are gagged open while such a torrent of water is poured in that it swells their bellies to great mounds, and then, being pierced with a spit or a similar sharp instrument, the belly spouts water through the hole, as a whale, when it has taken in the sea along with the herrings and other small fish of the sea, spouts water to the height of a plum tree. The pen, alas! is ashamed to narrate the enormities of the tortures elaborated for this purpose. The number and variety of them can scarcely be noted on a large parchment. The civil laws themselves extort the truth by similar tortures in criminal cases where sufficient witnesses are lacking, and many realms do likewise. But who is so hardy that, having once passed through this atrocious torment, would not rather, though innocent, confess to every kind of crime, than submit again to the agony of torture already suffered, and prefer to die once, since death is the end of terrors, than to die so many times and to suffer hellish torments more bitter than death?

[109] A royal ordinance of 1254 gave sanction to the use of torture as part of the judicial procedure in France, see Esmein, *Continental Criminal Procedure* (London 1914) 121–44. For details of the practice, see Dumont, *Justice Criminelle des Duchés de Lorraine et de Bar* (2 vols., Nancy, 1848).

[110] As with much of Fortescue's comparison, these remarks on the use of torture are aimed at English consciences. The rack was known as 'the duke of Exeter's daughter', the duke of Exeter being either Henry Holland (who was in exile with Fortescue in Bar or his father John Holland, both previously constables of the Tower), see Coke's *Institutes* (1628) 3.35, where it is also said that the duke of Exeter and the duke of Suffolk 'intended to have brought in the civil laws'. John Tiptoft, earl of Worcester and, from 1461 to 1467 and again in 1470, constable of the Tower and of England, who was also accused of introducing 'the law of Padua', is, however, probably the chief target, see Mitchell, *John Tiptoft*, 80 and see also J. Heath, *Torture and English Law. An Administrative and Legal History from the Plantagenets to the Stuarts* (London, 1982) ch. 3, esp. 49–57.

[111] This form of torture was known as 'strappado' in which the victim was hoisted up on a pulley with his hands tied behind his back and was then released and jerked to a halt again, see Dumont, *Justice Criminelle*, I, 83.

And, Prince, have you not heard of a certain criminal who, in the midst of such tortures as these, accused a worthy, honest, and faithful knight of treason to which he asserted they had together conspired, and who adhered to this story when released from the torment lest he should be put to torture again; but who nevertheless, when agonised by his pain, he was weakened to the point of death, and had at last taken his viaticum, the body of Christ, then swore by that body and by the death that he believed he was straight away to suffer, that the knight had been unblemished and innocent of all that of which he had accused him; the pain, he said, that he had endured at the time of his accusation had been so atrocious that, rather than experience it again, he would accuse the same knight once more, and indeed would accuse his own father, albeit he was now come to the threshold of death, which he believed he could no longer escape. Nor, indeed, did he evade the death which he then feared, but was at length hanged, and at the moment of his death he cleared the knight of every crime with which he had defamed him.[112]

Such confessions, alas! many other wretches make, not because of truth, but only because compelled by extreme torments. What certainty results from the confessions of people under such pressure? And if some innocent man, not forgetful of his eternal salvation even in such a Babylonian furnace as this, praises the Lord like the three boys,[113] and will not lie to the peril of his soul, so that the judge pronounces him innocent, does not the judge by such a judgement declare himself guilty of inflicting all that cruelty and pain on an innocent man? O! how cruel is a law such that when it is unable to convict the innocent, it condemns the judge himself! Truly, such a practice is not to be called a law, but is rather a pathway to hell. O judge, in what school did you learn to be present whilst the accused suffers agonies? In fact, judgements on criminals ought to be carried out by base creatures, for the executors of them become infamous by that very deed, whereby they are rendered unfit for judicial status. For the Lord executes His judgements on the damned not by angels, but by demons. And, indeed, in

[112] This reference dates the work to 1467–8 at the earliest, since it refers to the case of John Hawkins who, under torture, accused Sir Thomas Cook of treason in 1467, see Chrimes, *De laudibus*, 167; and Heath, *Torture and English Law*, 50–52.

[113] Daniel 3.

purgatory it is not good angels but evil ones who torment the souls who are none the less predestined for glory. Those men are also malign through whom the Lord visits the wretched in this world with the evil of pain. For when God had said in III Kings, chapter xxii, "Who shall entice Ahab for me?"[114] it was an evil spirit who answered, "I will be a lying spirit in the mouth of all his prophets."[115] For though the judgement that Ahab should be beguiled by a lie proceeded from the Lord, it was not fitting that a good spirit should carry into effect such a judgement.

But perhaps the judge has said, "I have had no hand in these tortures". Yet what is the difference between doing them with one's own hands and being present at them, and aggravating what is done again and again by his command? It is the master of a ship who alone brings her into port, though by his command others ply the helm. I believe that the wound that wounds the conscience of a judge who inflicts such tortures will never heal, especially whilst he remembers the agonies of pain of a poor wretch so afflicted.'

Chapter XXIII
Here he shows how often the civil law is deficient in justice

'Furthermore, if a right of action in a cause accrues to a man out of contracts, torts, or title of inheritance, the plaintiff will fail in his case if there are no witnesses, or if the witnesses are dead, unless he can prove his right by circumstantial evidence – which does not often happen. The same applies to actions concerning lordships and other possessions regulated by the civil law, and in all actions under the same law, plaintiffs are often non-suited for lack of evidence, so that scarcely one half are brought to the desired end. I doubt whether a law of this kind, which is so deficient in rendering justice to injured parties, is to be called just, since it is written in the same law that justice gives to everyone that which is his own which such a law as this does not.'

---

[114] I Kings 22:20.
[115] I Kings 22:22.

Chapter XXIV
Here he teaches how counties are distinguished and sheriffs are chosen

'Its having now been explained how the civil laws instruct the judge as to the truth of a fact brought to trial, it remains to explain how the laws of England elicit the truth of such a fact. For, if the principles of the two laws are set alongside each other, their qualities will stand out more clearly, since, as Aristotle says, "Opposites placed in juxtaposition are more manifest."[116] But here, in the place of a preface in the manner of orators, it will be fitting to mention first some points, an understanding of which will clarify matters yet to be treated. Wherefore we proceed thus.

The kingdom of England is distinguished into counties, as the kingdom of France is distinguished into bailiwicks, so that there is no place in England that is not within the body of some county. Counties also are divided into hundreds, which in some places are called wapentakes. Hundreds, again, are divided into vills, under which name boroughs and cities are included, for the boundaries of vills are not marked by walls, buildings or streets, but by the confines of fields, large tracts of lands, certain hamlets, and many other limits, such as watercourses, woods and wastelands, which it is not now necessary to designate, because there is scarcely any place in England that is not contained within the ambits of vills, though there are certain privileged places within vills which are not held to be part of those vills.[117]

Furthermore, in every county there is a certain single officer, called the king's sheriff, who, among other duties of his office, executes all commands and judgements of the king's courts to be executed in his county; his office is annual, and he is not allowed to officiate after one year, nor may he resume the same office for two years following. This officer is chosen thus. Every year on the day after All Souls there meet in the king's exchequer all his counsellors, as well the lords spiritual and temporal as all other justices,

---

[116] *Auctoritates*, 267, from Aristotle, *Rhetoric*, III. ii 1405a12–13. The Latin in *Auctoritates* has 'contraria' rather than Fortescue's 'opposita'.

[117] See Plucknett, *Concise History*, ch.1 and B. Guenée, *States and Rulers in later Mediaval Europe*, 111–14.

all the barons of the exchequer, the clerk of the rolls, and certain other officers, where all these, by common assent, nominate three knights or esquires of every county whom they think to be of better disposition and repute among the others of the county, and better fitted for the office of sheriff of the county; from these the king chooses one only, whom by his letters patent he constitutes sheriff of the county for which he is so chosen for the year following. But before he receives his letters, he shall swear upon God's holy gospels that, among other things, he will exercise and perform his office during the whole year properly, faithfully, and impartially, and that he will accept nothing by colour or reason of his office from anyone but the king.[118] These matters having been premised, let us proceed to the examination of those which we seek to know about.'

Chapter XXV
How jurors ought to be chosen and sworn[119]

'As often as the parties in the courts of the king of England come to an issue of the plea upon a matter of fact, the justices write by means of a royal writ to the sheriff of the county in which the fact is supposed to have occurred, ordering him to cause to come before the same justices, on a certain day prescribed by them, twelve good and lawful men of the neighbourhood where the fact is alleged, who stand in no relation to either of the parties at issue, to declare upon their oaths whether the fact be such as one of those parties says or

---

[118] 14 Edward III st.1, ch.7 (*Rot. Parl.* ii) prescribed the method of selection and limited the holding of the office of sheriff to one year. 1 Richard II ch.10 (*Rot. Parl.* iii) forbade re-election within three years. Other regulatory statutes include 4 Henry VI ch.1 and 8 Henry VI ch.9 (*Rot. Parl.* iv) but 23 Henry VI stated that previous legislation was not being observed, for example, in some cases people were holding office for ten years at a time. Sheriffs were crucial to the administration of local justice because it was they who executed writs and empanelled juries. Fortescue clearly knew of these abuses in the system as he was among the justices sent to investigate the circumstances surrounding the appointment of sheriffs in Lincolnshire in 1455–6. The report made on this occasion which was critical of the King's actions is printed in Chrimes, *De laudibus*, 170. Chrimes also prints the sheriff's oath at 171.

[119] The chapter headings here show clearly that this was not how things were, but how they 'ought to be'. For the very many problems associated with the administration of justice in the localities, see J.G. Bellamy, *Bastard Feudalism and the Law*, ch.1 'Sheriffs, Justices and Juries'.

not, as the other party avers.[120] On the appointed day the sheriff shall return the said writ before the justices, together with a panel of the names of those whom he has summoned for the purpose. Either party can challenge these (if they come) by saying that the sheriff made the panel favourable to the other party, that is, of persons not altogether impartial. If this exception is found true by the oath of two of the men selected, by the justices, for this purpose from the panel, the panel shall then be quashed, and the justices shall write to the coroners of the same county ordering them to make a new panel.

When this has been done, if that is similarly found to be faulty, it too shall be quashed; and then the justices shall choose two from among the clerks of the court, or others of the same county, who in the presence of the court shall on oath make an impartial panel, which shall be challenged by neither party. But when those thus empanelled come into court, either party can make an exception against any person among them (as he can in every case and every time when any of those on the panel, however empanelled, appears in court to swear upon the truth of an issue) by alleging that the empanelled person is related by blood or affinity to the other party or connected with him by friendship of any sort, and that he is not an impartial person for showing the truth between them.

Of these exceptions there are so many kinds and varieties that it is impossible to explain them in this short speech.[121] If any of these are found to be true, then he against whom the exception is taken shall not be sworn, but his name shall be cancelled from the panel. So also shall it be done with all the names on the panel until there are sworn twelve of them, so impartial that neither party has any matter of exception or accusation against them. But of those twelve at least four shall be of the hundred in which the vill is situated wherein the fact at issue is alleged to have occurred; and each of the jurors shall have lands or rents for the term of his life to the value of at least forty shillings a year. And this procedure is

---

[120] 42 Edward III ch.11 (*Rot. Parl.* II) was supposed to regulate the empanelling of jurors, but the whole system was subject to massive abuses. Bellamy (*Bastard Feudalism and the Law*, 9) states that the two types of criminal jury were particularly at risk at this time from novel civil law influences.

[121] For a discussion and examples of exceptions, see Plucknett, *Concise History*, 409–10.

observed in all actions and causes, criminal, real, and personal, unless the damage or debt in personal actions does not exceed forty marks of English money, because in such cases jurors are not required to be able to expend so much. They shall nevertheless have lands or rents to a competent value at the discretion of the justices, otherwise they shall not be sworn, lest through their hunger and poverty they may be easily corrupted or suborned.[122] And if through such exceptions so many names of jurors are cancelled from the panel that a sufficient number does not remain to make the jury, then the sheriff shall be commanded by a royal writ to appoint more jurors, which is often done lest the inquisition of truth of the issue of the plea shall not remain for lack of jurors. And this is the form in which jurors and inquisitors of truth of this kind ought to be chosen and sworn in the king's court. Now it remains for us to enquire how they ought to be charged and informed for their stating of the truth.'

Chapter XXVI
How jurors ought to be informed by evidence and witnesses

'Twelve good and lawful men, neither suspected by nor hostile to either party, but neighbours to them, having at length been sworn in the form aforesaid, and having as aforesaid sufficient possessions over and above moveables with which to maintain their status, the whole record and process of the plea pending between the parties shall be read to them by the court in English, and the issue of the plea, the truth of which they are to certify to the court, shall be clearly explained to them. Thereupon, each party, either by himself or by his counsel, shall declare and explain to these jurors in the presence of the court, all and singular witnesses whom he desires to produce for his own case. These witnesses, charged by the jus-

---

[122] Subornation refers to the abuses of embracery (bribing jurors) and labouring (influencing jurors or officers). Fortescue himself explained the difference between illegal and 'justifiable' maintenance and between legal informing and illegal 'labouring' during a case in 1450, see 'Legal Opinions and Judgements of Sir John Fortescue as Lord Chief Justice of England' in Clermont edn, 13. Conviction for these offences was rare, see Bellamy, *Bastard Feudalism and the Law*, 13–33.

tices, shall testify on God's holy gospels all they know concerning the truth of the issue about which the parties contend. And if need be, the witnesses shall be separated until they have deposed all they wish, so that the evidence of one of them shall not inform or induce another to testify in the same manner.

All this having been done, the jurors shall then confer together at their pleasure as to the truth of the issue, deliberating as much as they wish in the custody of the ministers of the court, in a place assigned to them for the purpose, lest in the meantime anyone should suborn them. Then they shall return into court, and certify to the justices the truth of the issue just joined, in the presence of the parties, if they desire to be present, particularly the plaintiff.

The statement of the jurors is called by the laws of England a 'verdict'. Then, according to the tenor of the verdict, the justices shall render and formulate their judgement. Nevertheless, if the other party, against whom the verdict has been brought, holds himself unjustly aggrieved by it, that party may sue out a writ of attaint against the jury and the party who obtained the verdict. In virtue of this writ, if it shall be found (by the oath of twenty-four men returned, chosen, and sworn in the form aforesaid, but having much greater patrimony than the first jurors) that those first jurors made a false oath, then the bodies of those jurors shall be committed to the prison of the lord king; their goods confiscated, and all their possessions seized into the king's hand; their houses and buildings demolished, their woods cut down, their meadows ploughed up, and they themselves shall henceforth be infamous, and their testimony as to the truth shall nowhere be accepted. The party who failed in the earlier trial shall then be restored to all that he lost on that occasion.[123] Who, then, even if he be unmindful of the safety of his soul, will not, having been sworn, speak the truth, in fear of so great a penalty and in shame of such deep infamy? And if perchance one amongst them does not hesitate to be so prodigal of his honour, yet some among so many jurors will not neglect their reputation nor suffer their goods and possessions to be distrained on account of his guiltiness.

Now, is not this procedure for revealing the truth better and more effective than the process which the civil laws devise? Here

---

[123] 15 Henry VI ch.5 (*Rot. Parl.* IV) and see Bellamy, *Bastard Feudalism and the Law*, 29.

none lose their case or right through the death or lack of witnesses; here no unknown witnesses are produced – no unreliable hirelings, paupers, vagrants, nor any whose condition and cunning is unknown. These 'witnesses' are neighbours, able to live of their own, sound in repute and fair-minded, not brought into court by either party, but chosen by a respectable and impartial officer, and compelled to come before the judge. These know all that the witnesses admit in their depositions, and they know the constancy, inconstancy, and repute of the witnesses brought forward. What more? Truly, nothing is omitted that can discover the truth of the question in dispute; nothing, provided it be within human apprehension, can be concealed from or unknown to such jurors.'

Chapter XXVII
Here he shows how criminal cases are determined in England

'But it is now very necessary to enquire how the laws of England examine the truth in criminal cases, so that the form of the laws being clearly apprehended, we can know for certain which more effectively reveals the hidden truth. If any suspected person in England, accused of felony or treason, denies his crime before the justices, the sheriff of the county where the deed was done shall cause to come before those judges twenty-four good and lawful men of the neighbourhood of the vill where the deed was done, who are related to the accused by no affinity, and each of whom has a hundred shillings of land or rents,[124] to certify to the judges as to the truth of that crime. All this having been done, the accused man can challenge them in the form described above as that which ought to be used in real actions. And further, the accused can challenge, in favour of his own life, the thirty-five men most feared by him, who at his challenge shall be cancelled from the panel, or marked by signs so that, to use the language of the law, they shall not pass upon him, even though he knows no cause to give for his exception and challenge.[125]

---

[124] Chrimes (*De laudibus*, 176–7) states that this is either a 'mistake' since the correct figure is 40 shillings, or that a reference to 21 Edward I has 'dropped out of the text'.

[125] See Plucknett, *Concise History*, 127–8, and in general, see Bellamy, *Criminal Law and Society*, ch. 3.

Who, then, in England can die unjustly for a crime, when he can have so many aids in favour of his life, and none save his neighbours, good and faithful men, against whom he has no manner of exception, can condemn him? I should, indeed, prefer twenty guilty men to escape death through mercy, than one innocent to be condemned unjustly. Nevertheless, it cannot be supposed that a suspect accused in this form can escape punishment, when his life and habits would thereafter be a terror to them who acquitted him of his crime. In this process nothing is cruel, nothing inhuman; an innocent man cannot suffer in body or members. Hence he will not fear the calumny of his enemies because he will not be tortured at their pleasure. Under this law, therefore, life is quiet and secure. Judge, therefore, O excellent Prince, which of these laws would be the best choice for you, if you hoped to live a private life.'[126]

Chapter XXVIII
The Prince concedes that the laws of England are more desirable to the subjects than the civil laws in the case already discussed

The Prince replies, 'I see no difficulty, Chancellor, to make one hesitate or waver in the choice which you put to me. For who would not choose to live under a law which makes it possible to live a secure life, rather than under such a law which always renders him weak and defenceless against the savagery of all his enemies? Indeed that man cannot be safe in body or goods, whom his enemy can in every cause convict by two, even unknown witnesses, chosen and brought forward by him. And even if he is not condemned to death by their evidence, yet he who escapes death is not much better off, considering the contraction of his sinews and limbs, and the chronic weakness of his body. Indeed, the cunning of an enemy can pursue with such danger a man who lives under the law which you have just described. But witnesses cannot work such evil when they make their deposition in the presence of twelve trustworthy men of the neighbourhood in which the fact in question occurred, knowing the

---

[126] This is not, as we have seen, a choice that he really has, but if he were to live a private life he *would choose* it; this is the idea of do unto others as you would be done unto.

circumstances and also the habits of the witnesses, especially if they are neighbours and cannot but know if they are worthy of credence. For whatever is done by or among their neighbours cannot be entirely hidden from all those twelve jurors. For example, I myself know more certainly what is now done in England than what has been done here in Bar where I at present reside.[127] Nor do I think it possible for that which is done, near his home, even with some secrecy, to escape the notice of an honest man. But still I wonder very much why this law of England, so fitting and so desirable, is not common to all the world.'

Chapter XXIX
Why inquisitions are not held by twelve sworn men in other kingdoms as in England

The Chancellor: 'You were a youth when you left England, Prince, so that the nature and quality of that land are unknown to you, but if you had known them, and had compared the products and character of other countries with them, you would not wonder at those things that puzzle you now. England is indeed so fertile that, compared area to area, it surpasses almost all other lands in the abundance of its produce.[128] It is productive of its own accord, scarcely aided by man's labour, for its fields, plains, glades, and groves abound in vegetation with such richness that they often yield more fruits to their owners uncultivated than ploughed lands, though those are also very fertile in crops and corn.

Moreover, in that land, pastures are enclosed with ditches and hedges and planted over with trees, by which the flocks and herds are protected from the wind and the sun's heat and most of them are irrigated, so that the animals, shut in their pens, do not need watching by day or by night. For in that land there are neither wolves, bears, nor lions, so the sheep lie by night in the fields without guard in their cotes and folds, whereby their lands are fertilised. Hence, the men of that land are not very much burdened with the

---

[127] This sentence does not appear to support what Fortescue is trying to say. Indeed, editors previous to Chrimes have inverted it, with no justification from the MSS.

[128] The description of England as a pastoral haven, bursting with all of the fruits of the earth has precedents in Geoffrey of Monmouth's *History of the Kings of Britain* and Bede's *Ecclesiastical History*.

sweat of labour, so that they live more spiritually, as the ancient fathers did, who preferred to tend flocks rather than to distract their peace of mind with the cares of agriculture. For this reason the men of that land are made more apt and disposed to investigate causes which require searching examination than men who, immersed in agricultural work, have contracted a rusticity of mind from familiarity with the soil.

Again, that land is so well stocked and replete with possessors of land and fields that in it no hamlet, however small, can be found in which there is no knight, esquire, or householder of the sort commonly called a franklin, well-off in possessions; nor numerous other free tenants, and many yeomen, sufficient in patrimony to make a jury in the form described above.

Furthermore, there are various yeomen in that country who can spend more than six hundred scutes a year,[129] so that juries in that country are often made up, especially in important causes, of knights, esquires, and others, whose possessions exceed two thousand *scutes* a year in total. Hence it is unthinkable that such men could be suborned or be willing to perjure themselves, not only because of their fear of God, but also because of their honour, and the scandal which would ensue, and because of the harm they would do their heirs through their infamy. Not any other kingdoms of the world, king's son, are disposed and inhabited like this. For although in them there are men of great power, great wealth and possessions, yet not one of them lives close to another, as so many do in England, nor does so great an abundance of heirs and possessors of lands exist as is to be found there.

For in those other countries in scarcely a single town can one man be found sufficient in his patrimony to serve on a jury. For, outside cities and walled towns, it is rare for any except nobles to be found who are possessors of fields or other immovables. There, again, the nobles do not have an abundance of pastures, and it is not compatible with their status to cultivate vineyards or to put hands to a plough, though the substance of their possessions consists in vineyards and arable, except only meadows adjoining large rivers and woods, the pasture of which is common to their tenants and neighbours.

---

[129] Scute probably refers to the French gold coins called *écus*. Six scutes were equivalent to one pound sterling.

How, then, can a jury be made up in such regions from among twelve honest men of the neighbourhood where the fact is brought into trial, when those who are divided by such great distance cannot be deemed neighbours? Indeed, the twelve jurors there will be very remote from the fact, after the accused in those regions has challenged, without cause shown, the thirty-five nearer ones. Thus it would be necessary in those countries to make a jury either of persons so remote from the fact in dispute that they do not know the truth about it, or of paupers who have neither shame of being infamous nor fear of the loss of their goods, since they have none, and are also blinded by rustic ignorance so that they cannot clearly perceive the truth.

'Do not wonder, therefore, Prince, if the law by which the truth is sought in England is not common to other nations, for they cannot, like England, make adequate and similar juries.'

Chapter XXX
The Prince here commends the laws of England in respect of their procedure by juries

Then the Prince says, 'Though we have said that comparisons are odious, nevertheless the civil law in the comparison made by you is delivered from all blame, because, though you have preferred the law of England to it, yet it does not deserve odium, since you have not disparaged it or its makers, but have shown only that the land where it rules is the cause of its not eliciting the truth in disputes by as good a procedure as the law of England does. We cannot dispute that the law of England is, indeed, in the case now discussed, more suitable for that realm than the civil law and we have no desire to exchange it for the civil law. Yet still this superiority of the law of England does not spring from the defects of the other law, but is caused only by the fertility of England.'

Chapter XXXI
The Prince is uncertain as to whether procedure by jury is repugnant to divine law

'But, Chancellor, though the form in which the laws of England reveal the truth in disputes pleases us not a little, yet we are rather doubtful whether that method is repugnant to holy scripture or not. For the Lord said to the Pharisees, John, chapter viii, "It is written in your law that the testimony of two men is true",[130] and approving this, the Lord said, "I am one who bears witness of myself, and the Father that sent me bears witness of me."[131] Since the Pharisees were Jews, to say that it is written in your law is to say that it is written in the law of Moses, which was given by the Lord through Moses to the children of Israel. Hence to be contrary to this law is to break the divine law, and hence it follows that the law of England, if it differs from this law, differs from the divine law, to which resistance is not permissible. It is also written, Matthew, chapter xviii, that the Lord, speaking of fraternal correction, among other things said, "If your brother will not hear you, take with you one or two more, that in the mouth of two or three every word may be established."[132] If in the mouth of two or three the Lord will establish every word, we seek without reason the verdict of more men in disputes. For no one can lay a better or other foundation than our Lord has laid. These are the matters, Chancellor, that somewhat disquiet me in the procedure of proof in the law of England. Therefore, I desire to know your answer to them.'

Chapter XXXII
Here he shows that procedure by juries is not repugnant to divine law

The Chancellor: 'The laws of England, Prince, are not contrary to these things which trouble you, though, in some measure, they elicit otherwise the truth in disputes. How does that law of a general council prejudice the testimony of two men, when it forbids the conviction of cardinals for crimes except by the deposition of twelve witnesses?[133] If the witness of two is true, *a fortiori* the testimony of twelve ought to be judged true; as a principle of the civil law says, the greater always contains in itself the lesser. The amount of

---

[130] John 8:17.
[131] John 8:18.
[132] Matthew 18:16.
[133] This is inaccurate: Gratian on C. 3, C II, q.4 states that two witnesses suffice regardless of the rank of the Cardinal.

his expenditure in caring for the wounded man was promised to the innkeeper, if it were more than the two pence he received.[134] Shall not a man who strives to prove he was absent for the time of the crime attributed to him produce more than two or three witnesses, when his accuser has proved or is prepared to prove his presence by two or three witnesses? Thus whosoever tries to convict witnesses of perjury must produce many more than these, for the testimony of two or three men will not always be judged true.[135] But that law is to be understood to mean that the truth in disputes ought not to be ascertained by witnesses fewer than two in number, as appears from Bernard, *Liber Extra de testimonio, cap. licet in Glossa ordinaria*, where he marks out various cases in which it is necessary, by the laws, to produce more than three witnesses, namely, in some of them five and in others seven.[136]

Again, the laws of England certainly affirm that the truth may be proved by two witnesses, when it is not otherwise made known. For if anything is done on the high sea outside of the body of any county of the realm, which is afterwards brought to trial before the admiral of England, it ought, by the rules of the laws of England, to be proved by witnesses.[137] The same procedure is customary before the constable and marshal of England, in cases concerning a fact occurring in another realm, if cognisance of it pertains to the jurisdiction of the court of the constable;[138] also in courts of certain liberties in England, which proceed by the law merchant, contracts among merchants made outside the realm are proved by witnesses. This is because in these cases neighbours, by whose oath juries of twelve men can be made, are not to be found, as is customary in contracts and other cases arising in the kingdom of England. Similarly if a charter, in which witnesses are named, is brought into the king's court, there will be process against those witnesses, and they also will declare on oath at the same time as twelve jurors, whether the charter is the deed of him whose it is alleged to be, or not.

Hence the law of England does not condemn the law by which the truth is obtained from witnesses, especially when necessity

---

[134] Luke 10:35.

[135] See Plucknett, *Concise History*, 436–7.

[136] Bernard of Parma (d.1263), gloss on the *Liber Extra*, (known as *Glossa Ordinaria*) C.23, x, 2, 20, *ad verbum Quedam.*

[137] On the Court of Admiralty, see Plucknett, *Concise History*, 660–64.

[138] On the Court of the Constable and Marshal, see Plucknett, *Concise History*, 205.

requires it, because the laws of England themselves do the same not only in the cases noted, but also in certain others which need not be mentioned here. But that law never determines by witnesses alone a cause which can be decided by a jury of twelve men, since this is a better and more effective method for eliciting the truth than the method of any other law in the world, and further removed from the danger of corruption and subornation. Nor can this form of procedure ruin any cause through lack of witnesses; nor can the attestation of witnesses, if there were any, fail to have its due effect; nor can twelve men of this sort be perjured, when they are most severely punished for their crime, and the party aggrieved by their deposition still has his due remedy. These things are not done at the will and dictate of strange or unknown men, but by the oath of honest men worthy of credit, neighbours, whom the parties have no cause to challenge, and whose verdict they have no cause to distrust.

O! what horrible and detestable diversity often ensues from the method of proceeding by the deposition of witnesses! Will not anyone who contracts a clandestine marriage, and afterwards betroths himself before witnesses to another woman, be compelled in the contentious court to consummate that marriage; and afterwards be adjudged in the penitential court to cohabit with the first woman, if he be duly required; and will he not be obliged to do penance every time he deliberately cohabits with the other woman, even though in both courts the judge shall be one and the same man? Is it not in this case, as is written in Job, that "Leviathan's testicles are perplexed"?[139] Alas! they are indeed perplexed, for thenceforth he shall cohabit with neither woman nor contract with another, without prosecution in the courts of contention and of penance. Such an evil, inconvenience, and diversity cannot possibly happen in any case by the method and form of the procedure of the law of England, even if Leviathan himself were moved to bring it about. Do you not see now, most excellent Prince, that the more you criticise the laws of England, the more they shine?'

---

[139] This is an inaccurate rendering of Job 40:17 which states 'the sinews of his testicles are perplexed' and which refers not to Leviathan, but to Behemoth.

Chapter XXXIII
Why certain kings of England were not pleased with their laws

'I do see', the Prince says, 'and I consider that they excel among all the other laws of the whole world in the case which you have now explained. But we have heard that some of my ancestors, the kings of England, were little pleased with their laws, and strove to introduce the civil laws into the government of England, and tried to repudiate the laws of the land.[140] I am indeed extremely surprised at their counsel.'

Chapter XXXIV
Here the Chancellor shows the reason for the matter which the Prince queries

The Chancellor: 'You would not wonder, Prince, if you considered with an alert mind the cause of this attempt. For you have already heard how among the civil laws there is a famous sentence, maxim or rule, which runs like this, "What pleased the prince has the force of law."[141] The laws of England do not sanction any such maxim, since the king of that land rules his people not only royally but also politically, and so he is bound by oath at his coronation to the observance of his law.[142] This, certain kings of England bore hardly, thinking themselves therefore not free to rule over their subjects as the kings ruling only royally do, who regulate their people by the civil law, and especially by the aforesaid maxim of that law, so that they change laws at their pleasure, make new ones, inflict punishments, and impose burdens on their subjects, and also determine suits of parties at their own will and when they wish.

---

[140] Selden's note on this states 'I confess here I understand him not. What kings of England ever desired the civil laws of Rome?', 'Notes upon Sir John Fortescue' in *De laudibus legum Anglie* (London, 1616), fo 41. See J.H. Baker, *The Reports of Sir John Spelman* vol II, Introduction.

[141] *Lex regia* found in *CIC* including: *Institutes* I, 2, 6, and *Digest* I, 4, 1.

[142] This is a reference to the fourth clause of the coronation oath, added in 1308, in which the king swears to keep the laws and customs which king and people 'will have chosen (*elegerit*)', see P.E. Schramm, *A History of the English Coronation*, 75–9.

Hence those ancestors of yours endeavoured to throw off this political yoke, in order thus to rule only royally over their subject people, or rather to rage unchecked, not heeding that the power of the two kings is equal, as is shown in the aforesaid treatise *Of the Nature of the Law of Nature*,[143] nor heeding that it is not a yoke but a liberty to rule people politically, and the greatest security not only to the people but also to the king himself, and no small alleviation of his care.

In order that these things may appear more clearly to you, consult your experience of both governments; begin with the results of only royal government, such as that with which the king of France rules his subjects; then examine the practical effect of the royal and political government, such as that with which the king of England rules over his subject people.'

Chapter XXXV
The evil things that come from only royal government in the kingdom of France[144]

'Remember, most admirable Prince, that you saw, whilst you were travelling, how rich in produce the villages and towns of the kingdom of France are. But they are so burdened by the king of that land's men-at-arms and their horses, that you could be entertained in scarcely any of them except the great towns. There you learned from the inhabitants that those men, though they might be quartered in one village for a month or two, paid, or wished to pay, absolutely nothing for the expenses of themselves and their horses, and, what is worse, they compelled the inhabitants of the villages and towns on which they descended to supply them at their own charges with wines, meats, and other things that they required, and to obtain from neighbouring villages more expensive necessities than they found there. And if any declined to do so, they were quickly compelled through cudgelling to do it at once. Then these men, having consumed the victuals, fuel and fodder for their horses in one village, hastened to another, to lay it waste in the same manner, paying not a penny for any of their own necessaries nor

---

[143] *On the Nature of the Law of Nature*, I. xxvi, see Appendix A, below 133.
[144] With this and the following chapter, cf. *The Governance*, ch. 3 notes, 87–90.

those of their concubines, whom they always carried with them in great numbers, nor for shoes, hose, or other items of the same sort, even to the smallest strap; on the contrary, they made the inhabitants of the villages where they stayed pay all their expenses of every kind. This is done in every village and unwalled town in the whole of that country, so that there is not one small town which is free from this calamity, and which is not plundered by this abominable extortion once or twice a year.

Moreover, the king does not suffer anyone of his realm to eat salt, unless he buys it from the king himself at a price fixed by his pleasure alone. And if any poor man prefers to eat without salt rather than buy it at excessive price, he is soon compelled to buy as much salt at the king's price as is proportionate to the number of persons he supports in his home. Furthermore, all the inhabitants of that realm give to their king every year a quarter of all the wines that accrue to them, and every innkeeper a fourth penny of the price of the wines that he sells; and yet again all villages and towns pay to the king annually huge sums assessed on them for the wages of men-at-arms, so that the king's troops, which are always very numerous, are kept in wages every year by the poor of the villages, towns, and cities of the realm. In addition, each village always maintains at least two archers, and some more, sufficiently accoutred and equipped to serve the king in his wars as often as it pleases him to summon them, which he frequently does. Notwithstanding all these, other very heavy tallages are levied to the use of the king every year, on every village of the realm, from which they are relieved in not a single year.

Exasperated by these and other calamities, the people live in no little misery. They drink water daily, tasting no other drink except at solemn feasts. They wear frocks or tabards of canvas like sackcloth. They do not use woollens, except of the cheapest sort, and that only in their shirts under their frocks, and wear no hose, unless to the knees, exposing the rest of their shins. Their women are barefooted except on feast days; the men and women eat no flesh, except bacon lard, with which they fatten their pottage in the smallest quantity. They do not taste other meats, roast or boiled, except occasionally the offal and heads of animals killed for the nobles and merchants. On the contrary, the men-at-arms eat their poultry, so that they are left with scarcely their eggs for themselves to eat as a rare delicacy. And if anyone grows in wealth at any time, and is reputed rich among the others, he is at once assessed for the king's subsidy more than his neighbours, so that he is soon levelled to their poverty. This, unless I am mistaken, is the condition of the estate of the common folk in that region; yet the nobles are not thus oppressed with exactions.

But if any one of them is accused of crime, even by his enemies, he is not always called before an ordinary judge. But it often appears that he is examined in the prince's chamber or other private place, indeed sometimes only by messengers, and as soon as he is adjudged to be guilty, on the information of others and according to the king's conscience, he is thrust into a sack without any form of trial, and is thrown by the ministers of the provosts of the marshals into the river at night and drowned.[145] You have heard that a great many more men die in this way than stand convicted by due process of law. But still, what pleases the prince has the force of law, according to the civil laws. You have heard of other similar enormities, and of others worse, whilst you have been resident in France and near that realm – perpetrated in detestable and damnable fashion, by colour of no law but this. To detail these would be to prolong our dialogue too much.

Now let us consider what the effect of the political and royal law, which certain of your ancestors tried to exchange for the civil law, has brought about in the kingdom of England; so that, instructed by a knowledge of both laws, you will be able to decide from their effects which seems to you more worthy to be chosen; for Aristotle says, as was mentioned above, "Opposites placed in juxtaposition are more manifest".[146]

Chapter XXXVI
The good things that come from the political and royal government in the kingdom of England

'In the realm of England, no one billets himself in another's house against its master's will, unless in public hostelries, where even so

---

[145] The provosts of the marshals became permanent officers under Louis XI with powers concerning provost cases. There was no appeal from their judgement.
[146] *Auctoritates*, 267, see above n.116.

he will pay in full for all that he has expended there, before his departure.[147] Nor does anyone take with impunity the goods of another without the permission of the proprietor of them; nor, in that realm, is anyone hindered from providing himself with salt or any goods whatever, at his own pleasure and of any vendor. The king, indeed, may, by his officers, take necessaries for his household, at a reasonable price to be assessed at the discretion of the constables of the villages, without the owners' permission. But none the less he is obliged by his own laws to pay this price out of hand or at a day fixed by the greater officers of his household, because by those laws he cannot despoil any of his subjects of their goods without due satisfaction for them.[148] Nor can the king there, by himself or by his ministers, impose tallages, subsidies, or any other burdens whatever on his subjects, nor change their laws, nor make new ones, without the concession or assent of his whole realm expressed in his parliament.[149]

Hence every inhabitant of that realm uses at his own pleasure the fruits which his land yields, the produce of his cattle, and all the emoluments which he gains, whether by his own industry or that of others, from land and sea, hindered by the injuries and rapine of none, without obtaining at least due amends. Hence the inhabitants of that land are rich, abounding in gold and silver and all the necessaries of life. They do not drink water, except those who sometimes abstain from other drinks by way of devotional or penitential zeal. They eat every kind of flesh and fish in abundance, with which their land is not meanly stocked. They wear good woollen clothes; they have abundant bedding (which is woollen like the rest of their furnishings) in all their houses, and are rich in all household goods and agricultural equipment, and in all that is requisite for a quiet and happy life, according to their estate. They are not brought to trial except before the ordinary judges, where they are treated justly according to the law of the land. Nor are they examined or impleaded in respect of their chattels, or pos-

---

[147] On billeting, see W.S. McKechnie, *Magna Carta* (2nd edn, New York), 332–3.
[148] On purveyance, see McKechnie, *Magna Carta*, (2nd edn, New York) 329–32, 334–6.
[149] 1297 *De Tallagio Non Concedendo* in which consent to tallage was required from 'archbishops, bishops and other prelates, earls, barons, knights, burgesses and other free men', H. Rothwell (ed.), *English Historical Documents* (London, 1975), vol.III, 486.

sessions, nor arrested for crime of whatever magnitude and enormity, except according to the laws of that land and before the aforesaid judges.

These are the fruits which the political and royal government yields. From these things the practical effects of that law, which certain of your ancestors tried to cast aside, are clear to you. Above all, also, the effects of that other law appear to you, which they tried, with so much zeal, to introduce in place of that law. And this is so that by their fruits you shall know them. Was it not ambition, lust, licence, which your said ancestors preferred to the good of the realm, that incited them to this exchange? Consider, therefore, excellent Prince, other matters that follow.'

Chapter XXXVII
The combination of the merits of both governments

'St Thomas, in the book which he wrote for the king of Cyprus, *On Princely Government*, says that "the king is given for the sake of the kingdom and not the kingdom for the sake of the king."[150] Hence, all the power of a king ought to be applied to the good of his realm, which in effect consists in the defence of it against invasions by foreigners, and in the protection of the inhabitants of the realm and their goods from injuries and rapine by the native population. Therefore, a king who cannot achieve these things is necessarily to be adjudged impotent. But if he is so overcome by his own passions or by such poverty that he cannot keep his hands from despoiling his subjects, so that he impoverishes them, and does not allow them to live and be supported by their own goods, how much more impotent then is he to be judged than if he did not suffice to defend them against the injuries of others? Indeed, such a king ought to be called not only impotent, but also impotence itself, and he cannot be deemed free, being fettered with such heavy bonds of impotence.[151] On the other hand, a king is free and

---

[150] Only the first book and the first four chapters of the second book of *On Princely Government* are now thought to have been written by Aquinas; it was continued by Ptolemy of Lucca, known as pseudo-Aquinas. This is a reference to pseudo-Aquinas, *De Regimine Principum*, III. xi. Fortescue also used this in *On the Nature of the Law of Nature*, I. xxv and *Governance*, ch. 8.

[151] See n. 88, above p. 24.

powerful who is able to defend his own people against enemies alien and native, and also their goods and property, not only against the rapine of their neighbours and fellow-citizens, but against his own oppression and plunder, even though his own passions and necessities struggle for the contrary. For who can be freer and more powerful than he who is able to vanquish not only others but also himself? The king ruling his people politically can and always does do this.[152] Hence, Prince, it is evident to you, from the practical effects, that your ancestors, who sought to cast aside political government, not only could not have obtained, as they wished, a greater power than they had, but would have exposed their own welfare, and the welfare of their realm, to greater risk and danger.

Yet these things, which, as seen in their practical effects, seem to reproach the power of the king ruling only royally, do not spring from a defect in the law but from the carelessness and negligence of such governance. So that those powers are not inferior in dignity to that of the king regulating politically. Both are equal in power, as I have clearly shown in the treatise *Of the Nature of the Law of Nature* before mentioned.[153] But all these matters now discussed show very clearly that the power of the king ruling royally is more difficult to exercise, and less secure for himself and his people, so that it would be undesirable for a prudent king to exchange a political government for an only royal one. Hence the aforementioned St Thomas is deemed to wish that all realms of the earth were ruled politically.'[154]

Chapter XXXVIII
An interpellation by the Prince

Then the Prince says, 'I beg you, Chancellor, to excuse my having compelled you, by my questions, to digress so far from your proposition. For what I have noted from the occasion is very useful to me,[155] though it has kept you back awhile from your intended goal,

---

[152] 'Self-restraint' is provided by the law.

[153] *On the Nature of the Law of Nature*, see Appendix A.

[154] Aquinas, *On Princely Government*, I. vi.

[155] The Prince has learned that he has no choice; the purpose of the exercise is now to show the Prince that he must choose to will what is good and effective for justice in England – a reformed 'dominium politicum et regale'.

to which I beg you to hasten more quickly; and first, inform me, as you promised and began, of some other cases in which the judgements of the laws of England and the civil laws differ.'

Chapter XXXIX
A second case in which the civil laws and the laws of England differ in their judgements

The Chancellor: 'I will try, Prince, to show you, as you ask, certain other cases in which the aforesaid laws differ. But, indeed, I will leave the question of which of these laws is superior in its judgements not to my decision, but to yours.

The civil law legitimates children born before matrimony as well as after, and causes them to succeed to the parental inheritance.[156] But the law of the English does not allow children born out of wedlock to succeed, proclaiming them merely natural and not legitimate.[157] The civilians extol their law in this point, because they say that thereby the sin, through which otherwise the souls of the two parties would perish, is absolved by the sacrament of marriage. They also say that it is to be presumed that the parties contracted in their first intercourse to do that which subsequent marriage manifests. The Church also holds such offspring to be legitimate.[158] These, unless I am mistaken, are the three principal arguments by which they approve and defend their law.

These are answered by those learned in the law of England thus; in the first place they say that the sin of the first intercourse in such a case is not purged by subsequent marriage, though the punishment of the offenders is deservedly mitigated in some measure. They say, also, that these sinners repent by so much the less, the more they consider the laws favourable to such transgressors. By such a consideration they are rendered all the more disposed to commit the sin, and thereby neglect the commands not only of God but also of the Church. So this law not only participates in the guilt of the offenders, but also deviates from the very nature of a good law since law is a holy sanction commanding what is honest and

---

[156] *Institutes* 1.10.13; *CIC, Code* 5.27. 8, 10 and 11. See J.A.C. Thomas, *A Textbook of Roman Law* (Amsterdam, 1976), ch. xxxix.
[157] Statute of Merton 1237.
[158] *Tanta est vis, CIC, Code* 6.x.4, 17.

forbidding the contrary;[159] for this law does not forbid but rather invites wavering minds to do dishonest acts.

Nor can this law be defended by the fact that the Church holds such offspring as legitimate. For that tender mother gives dispensation in many things which she does not allow to be done; for the Apostle relaxed the bridle of virginity by way of dispensation, though he was unwilling to counsel such acts, because he wished that all, like himself, should remain virgins.[160] Far be it from such a mother to withhold her affection from her sons in these cases, when, urged by the encouragement of this civil law, they often fall into sin. And the Church understands from subsequent marriage that the contracting parties repent of the past and wish in future to remain together in matrimony.

But the law of England in this case operates to a far different effect, for it does not encourage sin, nor favour sinners, but deters them, and threatens them with punishment lest they sin. For, indeed, the allurements of the flesh need no encouraging; they need rather restraints, for the desires of the flesh are lustful and well-nigh unremitting. And man, since he cannot perpetuate himself individually, naturally wants to be perpetuated in his species, because all that lives desires to be assimilated to the first cause, which is perpetual and eternal. Hence it is that man has more pleasure in the sense of touch, by which his species is preserved, than in the sense of taste, by which the individual is preserved. Thus Noah, avenging himself on his son who uncovered his shame, cursed his grandson, the son of the guilty one, who was thereby more punished than he could be by a disaster of his own.[161]

Hence the law which punishes the progeny of the offender prohibits the sin more effectively than the law which punishes only the guilty. From this you may observe how zealously the law of England prosecutes illicit intercourse when it not only judges the offspring thereof illegitimate but also forbids them to succeed to the parental patrimony. Is not then this a chaste law? Does it not more powerfully and firmly repulse sin than the said civil law, which quickly and almost without penalty remits the sin of lust?'

---

[159] This is from the Accursian gloss to *CIC Institutes*, 1, 2, 3, *v. Lex* and is also in Bracton, *On the Laws and Customs of England*, 1, iii. See above n.14.
[160] I Corinthians 7:36.
[161] Genesis 9:20–27.

Chapter XL
Special reasons why bastards are not legitimated by subsequent matrimony in England

'Besides, the civil laws say that "your natural son is the son of the people".[162] Concerning which a certain poet writes thus, "To whom the people is father, his father is to him nobody and everybody; to whom the father is the people, he has no father."[163] And since such a child has not a father at the time of his birth, nature knows not how he can obtain a father after the fact. Hence if one woman with two fornicators gives birth to two sons, and one of those concubinaries afterwards marries her, which of these two sons is legitimated by that matrimony? Opinion can persuade, but reason cannot discover, since both these sons, deemed offspring of the people, did not at first know their parents. Therefore it would appear inconsistent that a son born in wedlock to the same woman, whose procreation could not be dubious, should have no share in the inheritance, and the son who does not know his father should displace him in the succession to his father and mother, especially in the kingdom of England, where the elder son alone succeeds to the paternal inheritance.[164] Moreover, a fair arbiter would consider it no less inappropriate, if the son born of disgrace should participate equally in the inheritance, which by the civil law is divided among the males,[165] with a son born of a lawful marriage-bed.

For St Augustine, in the sixteenth book of *The City of God*, writes thus, "Abraham gave all his property to his son Isaac, but to the sons of his concubines he gave gifts."[166] From which it seems to be intimated that not the inheritance but only necessary provision is due to the spurious issue. Thus, indeed, says he. But under the name spurious, Augustine denotes all illegitimate offspring, in the way holy scripture often does, which calls no-one bastard. Observe that Augustine and Abraham make no small difference between the succession of spurious issue and the sons of legitimate intercourse.

---

[162] *CIC, Institutes* 1.10.12.

[163] Cited as a proverb in J.Werner, *Lateinische Sprichwörter und Sinnsprüche des Mittelalters* (1912), 14.

[164] On primogeniture, see Plucknett, *Concise History*, 527–530.

[165] On civil law succession, see J.A.C. Thomas, *A Textbook of Roman Law* (Amsterdam, 1976), ch. XLVI.

[166] Augustine, *City of God*, XVI.34.

Moreover, holy scripture reproves all illegitimate offspring, saying in a metaphor, "The shoots of the spurious shall not take deep roots nor lay a firm foundation", Wisdom, chapter iv.[167] The Church also reproves them and it rejects them from holy orders, and though it gives dispensation to them, yet it does not permit them to be of any dignity in the Church of God. It is fitting, therefore, that the law of men should deprive of the benefits of succession those whom the Church judges unworthy of holy orders and rejects from all prelacy,[168] and those whom holy scripture deems inferior in birth to those legitimately procreated.

Gideon, mightiest of men, is reported to have begotten seventy sons in matrimony, and only one from a concubine; but that son of his concubine wrongfully killed all save one of those legitimate sons, Judges, chapter ix.[169] For in one bastard more cunning was found than in the sixty-nine legitimate sons. It is a common proverb that, "If a bastard is good, it comes to him by accident", that is to say, by special grace; "but if he is bad, it comes to him by nature." For the illegitimate offspring is deemed to contract corruption and blemish from the sin of his progenitors through no fault of his own, just as we all contract it greatly from the crime of our first parents, though in not so great degree. But bastards contract from their procreation a blemish other than that contracted by legitimate issue, for it is the culpable and mutual lust of both their parents that contrives their engendering, which is not wont to prevail in the lawful and chaste embraces of married couples.

The sin of such fornicators is mutual and common, and, thereby resembling the original sin, it more impresses itself upon the offspring than any sin committed otherwise by solitary sinners, so that the child deserves to be called the son of sin rather than the son of sinners. Hence the Book of Wisdom, distinguishing the two procreations, says of the legitimate one, "O how beautiful is chaste and unblemished procreation! For its memory is immortal, because it is acknowledged by God and by men."[170] The other indeed is not acknowledged among men, so that sons born of it are called sons of the people. Hence that book says of this other procreation thus,

---

[167] Wisdom 4:3 (Vulgate).
[168] *Decretal Gregor IX, lib. IV, tit. l, cap.* xviii, in A. Friedberg (ed.), *Corpus Iuris Canonici pars secunda: Decretalium Collectiones. Cf.* Deuteronomy 23.2.
[169] Judges 8:30–31 and 9:23–24.
[170] Wisdom 4:1 (Vulgate).

"All sons who are born of iniquity are, when questioned, witnesses of the lewdness of their parents", Wisdom, the same fourth chapter.[171] For being asked about their parents, they reveal their sin, even as the worthless son of Noah revealed his father's shame.[172] It is believed, therefore, that the man born blind, of whom the Pharisees said in John, chapter ix, "You were altogether born in sin",[173] was a bastard who was born totally in sin; and there was added – "And do you teach us?"[174] It seems they understood that a bastard is not disposed by nature, as a legitimate son is, to knowledge and virtue.

Therefore, that law which makes bastards by birth equal to legitimate offspring in their parental inheritance does not make the right distinctions, since the Church deems them unequal in God's inheritance, holy scripture likewise makes the difference in the aforementioned form, and nature distinguishes them in her gifts, marking natural children with a seemingly natural blemish, even though latent in their minds. Which, then, illustrious Prince, of these laws, the English or the civil, do you esteem and adjudge preferable in this matter?'

Chapter XLI
The Prince approves the law which does not legitimate those born before matrimony

The Prince: 'Surely that which more strongly casts out sin from the realm, and more securely preserves virtue in it. I think also those who are held to be unworthy by divine law and whom the church disregards in its benefices, and whom also nature judges more prone to sin, are to be deprived of some of the benefits of human law.'

Chapter XLII
The third case in which the aforesaid laws differ

The Chancellor: 'I think you judge rightly, so I will mention other cases in which these two laws differ. The civil laws decree that

---

[171] Wisdom 4:6 (Vulgate).
[172] Genesis 9:22.
[173] John 9:34.
[174] John 9:34.

"The issue always follows the mother";[175] so that, if a woman of servile condition marries a man of free condition, their offspring will be servile, and conversely, if a bondsman marries a free woman, he will beget none but free children. But the law of England adjudges the issue never to follow the condition of the mother, but always that of the father.[176] So that a free man engenders none but free children from a free woman, and also from a bondswoman; and a serf can beget in matrimony none but a serf. Which of these laws do you think is better in its judgements? The law is cruel that condemns the guiltless children of a free man to servitude. Nor less cruel, it is held, is the law that condemns the innocent children of a free woman to servitude.

The civilians indeed say that the civil laws are superior in these judgements of theirs. For they say that "An evil tree cannot bring forth good fruit, nor a good tree bring forth evil fruit."[177] And it is the judgement of all law that every plant belongs to the soil where it is planted; also the issue is much more certain of the womb that brought him forth than of the father that begat him. To these points the experts in the law of England say that the issue of a lawful bed knows its mother with no more certainty that it knows its begetter. For both laws which are now in contention say in unison that he is the father whom the nuptials indicate. Is it not, then, more convenient that the condition of the son should follow that of the father rather than that of the mother, when Adam says of married couples that "These two shall be one flesh",[178] which the Lord explaining in the Gospel said, "Now they are not two, but one flesh."[179] And since the masculine comprises the feminine, the whole flesh thus made one, ought to be referred to the masculine, which is more worthy. Wherefore the Lord called Adam and Eve, not Eve, but because they were one flesh, he called them both by the name of the man, namely, Adam, as appears in Genesis, chapter v.[180]

The civil laws themselves also say that women always glitter in the radiant beams of their husbands. Hence *C. Qui professione se*

---

[175] From the Accursian gloss to *CIC Code* 6, 7, 2. pr. *v.* 'filius'.
[176] See Pollock and Maitland, *The History of English Law Before the time of Edward I* (2nd edn, repr. Cambridge 1968) I, 422–3.
[177] Matthew 7:18.
[178] Genesis 2:24.
[179] Matthew 19:6.
[180] Genesis 5:2.

excusant, book X, *li, fi.* The text says thus, "We advance women by the honour of their husbands. We ennoble them in their offspring, and we decree for them vicariously in the courts, and we change their domicile."[181] But if they afterwards go to a husband of lesser rank, and are deprived of their previous dignity, let them follow the rank and domicile of the later husband. And since every child, especially the male, bears the name of the father, not of the mother, then whence can it come that the son should, because of his mother, lose his honour or change his father's rank, whose name he will none the less retain, especially when his mother reflects the honour and condition of his father, and when the honour and condition of the man is never degraded by the vice of his wife? The law indeed ought to be accounted cruel which without cause commits the son of a free man to servitude, and transfers the land, for which a free man, innocent of crime, has toiled to give title to his innocent son, to an unworthy stranger, and which besmirches the father's name with the taint of the son's servitude.

A law is also necessarily adjudged cruel, if it increases servitude and diminishes freedom, for which human nature craves. For servitude was introduced by man for vicious purposes. But freedom was instilled into human nature by God. Hence freedom taken away from man always desires to return, as is always the case when natural liberty is denied. So he who does not favour liberty is to be deemed impious and cruel. In considering these matters the laws of England favour liberty in every case. And though these laws adjudge him a serf whom a serf begets in marriage with a free woman, these laws cannot be held severe or cruel. For a woman who subjects herself in marriage with a serf, makes one flesh with him, whereby she, as the above written laws say, follows his condition, and, of her own free will and not by any legal obligation, makes herself his handmaid, and indeed a bondswoman, just as those do who render themselves as serfs in the king's courts, or sell themselves into servitude, without being compelled to do so. How then can the laws declare free a son whom such a mother has in such wise brought forth? For a man is never so subject to his wife, though she be the greatest lady, as this free woman is subject to this serf, whom she makes her lord; for the Lord says to every wife,

---

[181] *CIC, Code* 10.40.9.

"You shall be under the power of your husband, and he shall have dominion over you."[182]

And as for what the civilians say about the fruit of a good and an evil tree, is not every wife, of free or servile condition, according as her husband is? And in whose soil does a husband sow, when his wife is one flesh with him, if not in his own? What if he implants a sweet shoot into the stock of a sour tree, since the tree is his, will not the fruit, though for a time it savours of the tree, always be his? And also be of a sweet nature, as was the shoot which the lord of the tree grafted? Thus the offspring born of a woman is the progeny of the husband, whether the mother is free or servile.

Yet the laws of England ordain that the lord of a bondswoman married to a freeman without consulting her lord, though he cannot repudiate the marriage, for, as the Gospel says, "Whom God hath joined let no man put asunder",[183] shall recompense himself from the freeman for the whole damage which he sustains because of the loss of his bondswoman and her service.[184] Now this, I think, is the sum and form of the law of England in the case in point. How, then, Prince, does it strike you in this matter, and which of these laws do you deem more excellent and more worthy to be chosen?'

Chapter XLIII
The Prince approves the law by which the issue does not follow the mother

The Prince: 'Reason does not allow us to doubt that the law of the English is superior to the law of the Romans in this case. And to me that law is always the better which renders favour rather than rigour to the parties. For I recall a principle of the civil law which says thus, "It is right that harshness is restrained and favour amplified" '.[185]

The Chancellor: 'And rightly so indeed. I will refer to you, Prince, another case in which these laws conflict, and then, without much more ado, I shall desist, lest this troubling you with so many

---

[182] Genesis 3:16.
[183] Matthew 19:6 and Mark 10:9.
[184] This is from Littleton's *Tenures*, see *Coke on Littleton*, 102.
[185] This is from the Accursian gloss to *Digest* 14, 6, 9, 4, *v.* 'liberantur'.

differences is burdensome to you, and lest my too prolonged discourse begin to weary you.'

Chapter XLIV
The fourth case in which the aforesaid laws differ

'The civil laws commit the guardianship of minors to the next in blood, whether agnates or cognates;[186] that is, to each according to his degree and order in the succession to the ward's inheritance. The reason for this law is that no one will trouble to rear the minor more carefully and favourably than the next of blood. But the laws of England determine the guardianship of minors quite differently. For there, if an inheritance held in socage descends to a minor from any of his agnates, the minor shall not be in the guardianship of any agnate, but shall be in the ward of his cognates, that is, of his relations on his mother's side. And if an inheritance shall descend to him from the side of his cognates, then the minor together with his inheritance shall be in the guardianship of the nearest agnate, and not his cognate, until he shall become adult. For those laws say, to commit the care of a minor to him who is the next in succession to him is like committing the lamb to be devoured by the wolf.

But if that inheritance is held not in socage but by knight service, then by the laws of that land, the minor and his inheritance shall be in the ward neither of agnates nor cognates but of the lord of the fee, until the minor shall be of the age of twenty-one years.[187] Who, do you think, is better able and willing to instruct such a minor in military exercises, which by reason of his tenure he is required to perform for the lord of his fee, than the lord himself, to whom such services are owed by the minor? For he, in order that he may be better served by his tenant, will display diligent care, and is to be held more capable of instructing him in these matters than the rest of the youth's friends, who are perhaps rustic and inexpert in arms, especially if the patrimony is not large.

---

[186] *CIC, Novels*, 118, 5.
[187] Statute of Marlborough (1267), ch.17, see Littleton, *Tenures* (ed. Wambaugh), sec.123 and A.W.B. Simpson, *An Introduction to the History of the Land Law* (Oxford, 1961), 18–19.

And what is more useful to the minor, who by reason of his tenure will expose his life and fortune to the dangers of war in the service of his lord, than to be trained in military and warlike exercises whilst he is a minor, since he will not be able to shun such activities in mature age? And, indeed, it will be no small advantage to the realm for its inhabitants to be expert in arms. For, as the Philosopher says, "Everyone does boldly what he knows himself to be not deficient in."[188] Do you then not approve this law, king's son, and do you not extol it above the other law just described?'

Chapter XLV
Here the Prince commends the education of the orphan sons of nobles

The Prince: 'Indeed, Chancellor, I do praise this law more than the other. For in the first part of it which you noted, it provides more carefully for the security of the minor than the civil law. But I am even more pleased with the second part of it. For as a result of this, the sons of the nobles in England cannot easily degenerate, but will rather surpass their ancestors in probity, vigour, and honesty of manners, since they will be trained in a superior and more noble household than their parents' home, though perhaps the parents themselves were educated in a similar household. Even so, the parents' home will not be the same as the household of the lord, to whom both parents and minors owe service.

The princes of the realm, and other lords holding immediately of the king, ruled by this law, cannot so easily slip into lewdness or crudity, if when they are young orphans they are cared for in the king's household. Hence I praise highly the magnificence and grandeur of the king's household, for within it is the supreme public school (*gymnasium*) for the nobles of the realm, and a school of vigour, probity and manners by which the realm is honoured and will flourish, and be secured against invaders, and will be made formidable to the enemies and friends of the kingdom.[189] This ben-

---

[188] This is not in *Auctoritates*, but cf. below ch.LIV, 78.

[189] A decision of the council 28 June 1425 determined that all heirs minor of baronies-in-chief were to be educated at the king's expense in the king's household. This theme was later developed by English humanists, especially the common

efit, indeed, could not have accrued to the realm, if the sons of the nobles, orphans and minors were nurtured by the poor friends of their parents. Nor can it serve the good of the realm, if the sons of burghers and other free tenants who hold their tenements in socage, though not bound to military service, are educated in the homes of friends of like condition, as can clearly appear to anyone carefully considering it.'

Chapter XLVI
At this point he recites cases in which the aforesaid laws differ

Then the Chancellor: 'There are some other cases in which the said laws differ. Thus, the civil law adjudges a theft detected in the act to be expiated by a four-fold compensation, and a theft not detected in the act by a two-fold one.[190] But the laws of England allow neither act to be punished more lightly than by sentence of death, if the value of the article stolen exceeds twelvepence.[191]

'Again, the civil laws restore a thankless freedman to his former servitude,[192] but the laws of England adjudge a man once freed, grateful or ungrateful, always free.[193] There are also not a few more cases of this sort,[194] which I now pass over for the sake of brevity. Nor will I now describe the superiorities of the said laws in these two cases, since their qualities do not need close investigation. Nor do I doubt that the acuteness of your intelligence can sufficiently examine them.'

---

lawyer Sir Thomas Elyot and the civilian Thomas Starkey whose works stressed the importance of the building up of public allegiance, service to the common wealth and training for public office.

[190] *CIC, Institutes* 4.1.5, see Thomas, *A Textbook of Roman Law* (Amsterdam, 1976), ch.xxviii.

[191] See Pollock and Maitland, *The History of English Law Before the time of Edward I* (2nd edn, repr. Cambridge, 1968) I, 477.

[192] *CIC Institutes* 1.16.1, see Thomas, *A Textbook of Roman Law* (Amsterdam, 1976), ch.xxxv.

[193] Pollock and Maitland, *The History of English Law Before the Time of Edward I* (2nd edn, repr. Cambridge 1968) I, 428.

[194] See W.W. Buckland and A.D. McNair, *Roman Law and Common Law a Comparison in Outline* 2nd edn revised by F.H. Lawson (Cambridge, 1952).

Chapter XLVII
The Prince dismisses the cases just mentioned

The Prince: 'There is no need, Chancellor, to argue much in these cases. For though in England clandestine and open thieves are everywhere punished with death, they do not cease to plunder there, and if they do not in the least fear so great a penalty, how much less would they abstain from crime, if they anticipated a lesser punishment? And God forbid that a man once escaped from servitude should henceforth be perpetually under fear of a return to it, especially by reason of ingratitude, for the species of ingratitude can scarcely be numbered, they are so many, and human nature always demands in the cause of liberty more favour than in other causes. And now, Chancellor, I earnestly implore you to lay aside henceforth the examination of more cases of this sort, and to tell me why the laws of England, so good, fitting, and desirable, are not taught in the Universities, as the civil and also the canon laws are, and why in them the degrees of bachelor and doctor are not given, as they are usually given in other faculties and sciences.'

Chapter XLVIII
Here the Chancellor shows why the laws of England are not taught in the Universities

The Chancellor: 'In the Universities of England the sciences are not taught unless in the Latin language.[195] But the laws of that land are learned in three languages, namely, English, French, and Latin; in English, because among the English the law is deeply rooted; in French, because after the French had, by duke William the Conqueror of England, obtained the land, they would not permit the advocates to plead their causes unless in the language that they themselves knew, which all advocates do in France, even in the court of parliament there. Similarly, after their arrival in England, the French did not accept accounts of their revenues, unless in their own idiom, lest they should be deceived thereby. They took no pleasure in hunting, nor in other recreations, such as games of dice

---

[195] Some classes were conducted in French, see the Oxford statute of 24 May 1432, printed in Chrimes, *De laudibus*, 196.

or ball, unless carried on in their own language. So the English contracted the same habit from frequenting such company, so that they to this day speak the French language in such games and accounting, and were used to pleading in that tongue, until the custom was much restricted by force of a certain statute;[196] even so, it has been impossible hitherto to abolish this custom in its entirety, partly because of certain terms which pleaders express more accurately in French than in English, partly because declarations upon original writs cannot be stated so closely in the form of these writs as they can in French, in which tongue the formulas of such declarations are learned.

Again, what is pleaded, disputed, and decided in the royal courts is reported and put into book form, for future reference, always in French.[197] Also, very many statutes of the realm are written in French. Hence it happens that the language of the people in France now current does not accord with and is not the same as the French used among those learned in the law of England, but is commonly corrupted by a certain rudeness. That cannot happen with the French used in England, since that language is there more often written than spoken. In the third language above mentioned, that is, in Latin, are written all original and judicial writs, and likewise all records of pleas in the king's courts, and also certain statutes.

Thus, since the laws of England are learned in these three languages, they could not be conveniently learned or studied in the Universities, where the Latin language alone is used. But those laws are taught and learned in a certain public academy,[198] more convenient and suitable for their apprehension than any University. For this academy is situated near the king's courts, where these laws are pleaded and disputed from day to day, and judgements are rendered in accordance with them by the judges, who are grave men, mature, expert and trained in these laws. So those laws are read and taught in these courts as if in public schools, to which students of the law flock every day in term-time. That academy,

---

[196] 36 Edward III (*Rot. Parl.* II) st.1, ch.15.
[197] See Plucknett, *Concise History*, 268–273. On Year Books in the fifteenth century, see A.W.B. Simpson, *Legal Theory and Legal History; Essays on the Common Law* (London, 1987), 53–66.
[198] I have translated 'studium' as 'academy', but it is in many ways a more general expression, meaning simply 'a place of study'.

also, is situated between the site of those courts and the City of London, which is the richest of all the cities and towns of that realm in all the necessaries of life. And that academy is not situated in the city, where the tumult of the crowds could disturb the students' quiet, but is a little isolated in a suburb of the city, and nearer to the aforesaid courts, so that the students are able to attend them daily at pleasure without the inconvenience of fatigue.'

Chapter XLIX
Here he shows the general organisation of the academy of the laws of England

'But, Prince, in order that the form and likeness of this academy may be clear to you, I will now describe it as far as I can. For there are in this academy ten lesser inns, and sometimes more, which are called Inns of Chancery.[199] To each of them at least a hundred students belong, and to some of them a much greater number, though they do not always gather in them all at the same time. These students are, indeed, for the most part, young men, learning the originals and something of the elements of law, who, becoming proficient therein as they mature, are accepted into the greater inns of the academy, which are called the Inns of Court. Of these greater inns there are four in number,[200] and some two hundred students belong in the aforementioned form to the least of them. In these greater inns, no student could be maintained on less expense than twenty marks a year, and if he had servants to himself alone, as the majority have, then he will bear more expenses accordingly. Because of this costliness, there are not many who learn the laws in the inns except the sons of nobles. For poor and common people cannot bear so much cost for the maintenance of their sons. And merchants rarely desire to reduce their wares by such annual burdens. Hence it comes about that there is scarcely to be found in the realm a man

---

[199] The ten Inns of Chancery then extant were Barnard's, Chester, Clifford's, Farringdon, Furnival's, the Inner, Lyons, St George's, Scrope's and Staple, see H.H.L. Bellot, 'The Inns of Chancery, their Origin and Constitution', *Law Magazine and Review* xxxvii (1912).

[200] The four Inns of Court are Lincoln's, Gray's, Inner Temple and Middle Temple, see A.W.B. Simpson, 'The Early Constitution of the Inns of Court' in his *Legal Theory and Legal History; Essays on the Common Law* (London, 1987) 17–32.

trained in the laws, who is not noble or sprung of noble lineage. So they care more for their nobility and for the preservation of their honour and reputation than others of like estate.[201]

In these greater inns, indeed, and also in the lesser, there is, besides an academy of law, a kind of public school of all the manners that the nobles learn. There they learn to sing and to exercise themselves in every kind of harmonics. They are also taught there to practise dancing and all games proper for nobles, as those brought up in the king's household are accustomed to practise. In the vacations most of them apply themselves to the study of legal science, and on holy days to the study of holy scripture and, after the divine services, to the reading of chronicles. This is indeed a cultivation of virtues and a banishment of all vice. So for the sake of the acquisition of virtue and the discouragement of vice, knights, barons, and also other magnates, and the nobles of the realm place their sons in these inns, although they do not desire them to be trained in the science of the laws, nor to live by its practice, but only by their patrimonies.

Scarcely any turbulence, quarrels, or disturbance ever occur there, but offenders are punished with no other punishment than expulsion from participation in their mutual society, which is a penalty they fear more than criminals elsewhere fear imprisonment and fetters. For a man once expelled from one of these societies is never received into the fellowship of any other of those societies. Hence there is continual peace and their conduct is like the behaviour of such as are conjoined in perfect amity.[202]

It is not necessary to relate here the manner in which the laws are learned in these inns, for, Prince, you are not to experience it. But be assured that it is pleasant, and in every way suited to the study of that law, and also worthy of every regard. But I want you

---

[201] The author of the *Boke of Noblesse*, written in the 1450s to induce Henry VI to follow a policy of war rather than peace, recommends that young noblemen should 'be drawn forth, nourished and exercised in disciplines, doctrine and usage of the school of arms'. He goes on to bemoan the situation (of which Fortescue here proudly boasts) in which 'many who are descended of noble blood and born to arms ... set themselves to singular practice, ... as to learn the practice of law or custom of land, or of civil matters, and so waste greatly their time in such needless business', J.G. Nichols edn, 76–7.

[202] Fortescue's description presents the Inns as the 'forma et imago' of a perfect society; a mutual and voluntary society, eating together and combining elements of the active and contemplative life.

to know one point – that in neither Orléans, where the canon as well as the civil laws are studied, and whither students resort from all parts, nor Angers, nor Caen,[203] nor any other University of France,[204] except only Paris, are so many students of mature age to be found as in this academy, even though all the students there are of English birth alone.'

Chapter L
Of the estate and degree of the serjeant-at-law and how he is created

'But, Prince, since you wish to know why the degrees of bachelor and doctor are not given in the laws of England, as they are customarily given in both laws in the Universities, I want you to know that, though degrees of this kind are not conferred at all in the laws of England, yet there is given in them, not only a degree, but also a certain estate, not less eminent or solemn than the degree of doctor, which is called the degree of serjeant-at-law; and it is conferred in the following form.[205]

The chief justice of the common bench is accustomed, with the counsel and assent of all the justices, to choose, as often as seems to him opportune, seven or eight of the persons of mature age who have become more proficient in the laws in the aforesaid general academy, and who seem to the justices of the best disposition. Then he is accustomed to send their names in writing to the chancellor of England, who thereupon by writ of the king to each of those

---

[203] In 1219, the University of Orléans was granted, by Honorius III, authority to teach both civil and canon law. The University of Angers held classes, the students of which were known as *Justiniani*. The University of Caen was established in 1432 by John, duke of Bedford, under the authority of the letters patent of Henry VI and with the permission of Martin V, for the study of civil and canon law.

[204] These were Montpellier, Toulouse, Avignon, Cahors and Orange.

[205] Serjeants-at-law have 'status et gradus', they are not holders of royal office. J.H. Baker explains: 'at some time in the fourteenth century the choice of new serjeants came to be made, or at least confirmed, by the king. Yet the king never, at any stage in history, "appointed" serjeants in the true sense of the word, and serjeants were never regarded in law as officeholders. The serjeant's writ, which became a necessary preliminary to creation, was not a grant but an order to prepare to take a degree', *The Order of the Serjeants-at-Law*, 6.

chosen commands that he shall be before the king at a day assigned by him, to take upon himself the estate and degree of serjeant-at-law, under very heavy penalty fixed in each of the aforesaid writs. At the day assigned, each of them who appears shall swear on God's holy gospels that he will be ready, at a day and place to be determined for him, to receive the aforesaid estate and degree, and that on the day he will give away gold,[206] according to the custom of the realm used on this occasion.

But I omit to include here how each of those chosen is to conduct himself on that day, and the form and manner in which this estate and degree are conferred and received, for they need more writing than is fitting for so succinct a work. Besides, I have explained it to you in discussion at other times. But I want you to know that, on the day so fixed, those chosen are to hold, among other solemnities, a feast and entertainment[207] such as are held at the coronation of a king,[208] which lasts for seven days. Nor does anyone of those chosen complete the festivities contingent to the solemnity of his creation with less expense than four hundred marks, so that the expenditure, which all so chosen meet, exceeds in sum three thousand two hundred marks. A certain part of this, among other, will be expended in this way.

Each of them will give gold rings to the value in all of £40 at least in English money.[209] And your Chancellor himself well remembers that, when he had received this estate and degree, he spent £50, which are three hundred *scuta*, on rings which he distributed at that time. For each of these serjeants, at the time of his creation, customarily gives to each prince, duke, and archbishop

---

[206] Gower, in his *Mirour de l'Omme* (c.1380), said that this giving of gold signified that for the rest of their lives the serjeants would be taking gold back in even greater abundance, *Complete Works*, II, 269, see Baker, *The Order of the Serjeants-at-Law*, 17 and 35.

[207] By the end of the fourteenth century it was customary to hold a feast at the creation of the serjeants-at-law. These occasions consisted of seven days of wining and dining at Ely House or Lambeth Palace, see Baker, *The Order of the Serjeants-at-Law*, 99–101.

[208] See Schramm, *History of the Coronation*, 93–5.

[209] Gold rings with appropriate mottoes (for example, 'Rex est anima legis') were given out at each creation. The first detailed list of these which we have dates from the 1521 creation when 762 rings were given; the list is similar to Fortescue's but omits the Chamberlains, see Baker, *The Orders of the Serjeants-at-Law*, 94–8 and Appendix II.

present at that solemnity, and to the chancellor and treasurer of England, a ring of the value of eight scutes; and to each earl and bishop likewise present, and to the keeper of the privy seal, to both chief justices, and the chief baron of the king's exchequer, a ring to the value of six scutes; and to every baron of parliament, and every abbot and noble prelate, and great knight there present, and the keeper of the rolls of the king's chancery, and to each of the justices, a ring to the value of four scutes. Similarly to every baron of the king's exchequer, to the chamberlains and the officers and notable men serving in the king's courts, rings of lesser value suitable to the estates of the recipients, so that there will not be a clerk, especially in the court of common bench, even the most inferior, who shall not receive a ring proper to his degree. And besides, they give rings to some others of their friends. Likewise a great livery of cloth all of one suit, which they will distribute in great quantity, not only to their servants, but also to their friends and acquaintances who attend them and serve them at the time of the aforesaid solemnity.[210]

Hence, although in the Universities those admitted to the degree of doctor meet no small expense at the time of their creation, and bestow caps and gifts other than in kind, yet they do not give gold or other gifts or hold a feast comparable to these in cost.[211] Nor in any realm in the world is a special degree given in the laws of the realm, except only in the realm of England. Nor is there any advocate in the whole world who enriches himself by reason of his office as much as the serjeant. Again, none, though he be the most learned in the laws of the realm, will be installed in the office and dignity of a justice in the courts of pleas before the king himself and the common bench, which are the supreme ordinary courts of the realm, unless he shall have been first invested with the estate and degree of serjeant-at-law.

Nor shall anyone except such a serjeant plead in the court of the common bench, where all pleas of real property are pleaded. Nor has anyone been admitted to this estate and degree who has not first completed sixteen years at least in the aforesaid general academy of

---

[210] See Baker, *The Orders of the Serjeants-at-Law*, 90–91.

[211] For the ceremonies associated with university commencements, see Baker, *The Orders of the Serjeants-at-Law*, 91 and 95; and A.B. Cobban *The Medieval English Universities*, 370–72.

the law; and as a sign that all justices have so graduated, each of them, when seated in the court of the king, will wear a coif of white silk, which is the primary and principal of the distinctions of dress with which serjeants-at-law are decorated at their creation. Nor shall a justice or serjeant-at-law ever doff this coif, so that his head is entirely uncovered, even in the presence of the king, even though he is talking to his highness.[212]

So, most illustrious Prince, you cannot henceforth doubt that these laws are honoured not only above the civil laws in particular but also above the laws of every other realm, and are venerated by the solemn estate of those learned servants of them, and that they be valuable, noble and sublime, of great excellence, and of the highest science and virtue.'

Chapter LI
Of the manner of the creation of a justice, and of his dress and conduct

'But that the estate of the justices may be known to you, in the same way as that of the serjeants-at-law, I will now describe, as far as I can, their form and office.[213] There are usually five justices in the common bench, or six at most, and in the king's bench four or five; and when any of them vacates office by reason of death or otherwise, the king customarily chooses, by the advice of his council, one of the serjeants-at-law, and appoints him to the justiciary by his letters patent, in the place of the judge thus vacating; then the chancellor of England shall come to the court where the vacancy is, bringing with him those letters, and, seated in the midst of the justices, he shall cause the serjeant so chosen to be introduced, and notify him, in open court, of the king's will concerning the office

---

[212] The coifs were white silk close-fitting caps which tied under the chin. It is highly significant that the serjeants do not remove their head-covering in the presence of the king, for it symbolises the fact that they obey a higher order. The serjeants are 'character indelibis', that is, once created as serjeants, they survive even the demise of the king intact, unlike the justices, see Baker, *The Orders of the Serjeants-at-Law*, 89 and 51.

[213] The justices are appointed by letters patent, and on the demise of the king they revert to being serjeants-at-law until new patents are sealed, see Baker, *The Orders of the Serjeants-at-Law*, 51.

of judge then vacant, and shall have the said letters read in public. This being done, the keeper of the rolls of the king's chancery shall read before the justice-elect the oath which he is to take,[214] and when he has so sworn upon God's holy gospels, the chancellor shall give him the said letters of the king, and the chief justice of that court shall assign him a place in it, where he shall henceforth sit, and shall soon cause him to be seated there.

But you must know, Prince, that the justice shall swear among other things that he will do justice without favour, to all men pleading before him, friends and foes alike, that he will not delay to do so even though the king should command him by his letters or by word of mouth to the contrary. He shall swear also that he will not receive from anyone except the king any fee or other pension, or livery, nor take any gift from any pleaders before him, except food and drink of no great price. You ought to know that a justice so created shall not make an entertainment, solemnity, or any feast at the time of his taking office and dignity, for they are not any sort of degree in the faculty of law, but are only an office and magistracy, terminable at the will of the king. But he shall change his dress in certain particulars but not in all its distinctions.

For, when a serjeant-at-law, he was dressed in a long robe, like a priest's, with a furred cape about his shoulders, and above that a hood with two tappets, as doctors of law customarily wear in certain Universities, and with a coif above described. But having been made a justice, he shall wear, in place of a cape, a cloak fastened upon his right shoulder; he shall still retain the other ornaments of a serjeant, except that a judge shall not wear a striped or particoloured garment as the serjeant can, and his robe is edged with no other fur than minever, whereas the serjeant's is always furred with white lamb.[215] This dress I wish you would make more distinguished when you come into power, for the adornment of the estate of the law and the honour of your realm.

I also wish you to know that the justices of England do not sit in the king's courts except for three hours a day, that is, from eight o'clock in the morning till eleven, because those courts are not held

---

[214] Chrimes prints the justice's oath, *De laudibus*, 204.

[215] On the serjeants' and the justices' dress, see Baker, *The Orders of the Serjeants-at-Law*, 73–8. During the reign of Henry VIII the chief justice of Common Pleas told the new serjeants that the two tongues or tappets signified the equity of the law and the rigour of the law, see Baker, *The Orders of the Serjeants-at-Law*, 293.

in the afternoon. But pleaders then attend at the parvis[216] and else-where to confer with the serjeants-at-law and their other counsel. Hence the justices, after they have refreshed themselves, pass the whole of the rest of the day in studying the laws, reading holy scripture, and otherwise in contemplation at their pleasure, so that their life seems more contemplative than active. Thus they lead a quiet life, free of all worry and worldly cares. Nor was it ever found that any of them was corrupted by gifts or bribes.[217]

Thus we have seen their kind so perpetuated by grace that scarcely any of them die without issue, which is like a great and as it were appropriate benediction of God. I think it no less a divine gift that more leaders and magnates of the realm, who have made themselves rich, illustrious and noble by their own prudence and industry, arise from the issue of judges than from any other estate of men in the realm. Yet the estate of merchants, of whom some are richer than all the justices of the realm, exceed the justices in number by thousands. This cannot be ascribed to fortune, which is nothing, but, I think, is to be attributed only to the divine benediction. For the Lord says in the words of the prophet, "that the generation of the righteous shall be blessed",[218] and elsewhere the prophet says, speaking of the just, "their children shall be blessed".[219] Therefore, king's son, love justice which enriches, honours, and perpetuates the offspring of its followers. And be a zealot for the law, which is the parent of justice, in order that it may be said of you, what is written of the just, "and their seed shall endure for ever"'.[220]

Chapter LII
The Prince reproves the delays in the king's courts

The Prince: 'Now one point only remains, Chancellor, to be dis-posed of, which yet disquiets and disturbs my mind, and if you

[216] I have translated 'ad pervisam' as 'at the parvis' rather than 'in chambers' as Fortescue is probably referring to the parvis of St Paul's where lawyers frequently met their clients, see Baker, *The Orders of the Serjeants-at-Law*, 103.

[217] Chrimes here accuses Fortescue of having too short a memory but, as with all of the other abuses in the system, Fortescue could not have been unaware of the situation. He is consciously provoking reform. For examples of the corruption of judges, see *Rot. Parl.*, III 44, 101, 158, 423, 433, 623 and 639.

[218] Psalms 112:2.

[219] Psalms 37:26.

[220] Psalms 89:36.

settle it, I will not weary you with any more questions. The laws of England, as it is asserted, suffer huge delays in their processes, more so than the laws of other nations – delays which not only withhold petitioners from their right, but impose an intolerable burden of expense, especially in those actions in which damages are not awarded to plaintiffs.'

Chapter LIII
Delays in the king's courts are necessary and reasonable

The Chancellor: 'In personal actions, outside cities and market towns, where the procedure is according to the customs and liberties of the place, processes are normal, and suffer a certain amount of delay, but not excessively. In cities and those towns, indeed, when urgent cause strongly requires, process becomes as quick as in other parts of the world,[221] yet they are not so hurried, as elsewhere, that one of the parties suffers injury.

Again, in real actions, in almost all parts of the world, process is slow, but in England is somewhat more speedy. There are, to be sure, in the high court of the kingdom of France, which is called the court of parliament, certain actions which have been pending for more than thirty years. I myself know one case of appeal which was begun in that court, between Richard Heron (an English merchant) and other merchants,[222] of trespass done within the jurisdiction of that court, and has now been adjourned these ten years, and very likely cannot be decided within another ten years. When I was staying in Paris, my host showed me his process in writing, which he had sued out in the court of parliament there eight years before for four *soliditis* which in our money scarcely exceeds eight *denarii*; and he had no hope of obtaining judgement within another eight years.[223] I know also some similar cases there.

---

[221] For example in the courts of piepowder, see Plucknett, *Concise History*, 660.

[222] This case is also mentioned in Fortescue's 'memo' to Louis XI. For full details, see H.G. Richardson, 'Illustrations of English History in the Medieval Registers of the Parlement of Paris', *TRHS* 4th ser. X (1927) 55–85.

[223] This appears to be at least as much an attack on excessive litigiousness as on delays in procedure. Fortescue made at least two trips to Paris during his exile at St Mihiel – one in 1464 and the other in 1470.

So it seems to me that the laws of England do not admit of such delays as the laws of that country. But, indeed, it is most necessary for delays to be made in the process of all actions, so long as they are not too excessive. For by such delays the parties, especially the defendants, can often provide themselves with useful defence and counsel, which they would otherwise lack. Nor is danger ever so likely in judgements as when process is hurried. I once saw in the city of Salisbury, before a certain judge of gaol-delivery, with clerk assigned to him, a woman convicted and burnt for the death of her husband within a year of his murder. In this case the judge could have respited the charge or proof against the woman until after that year. And, when the year was over, I saw a servant of the dead man convicted of the murder of his master before the same justice, a servant who then publicly confessed that he alone killed his master, and that his mistress, the wife, who had been burnt, had been entirely innocent of his death; whereupon he was drawn and hanged. But still, at the point of death, he mourned his burnt mistress, who had been innocent of that crime. O what sort of pang of conscience and remorse we must imagine, because of this deed, to have come to this so hasty a judge, who could have rightly stayed execution! Often, alas! he has told me, that never in his life would he purge his mind of that deed of his. For judgements may often mature through deliberation, but never by over-hasty procedure.

Hence the laws of England admit essoin,[224] such as the laws of the rest of the world do not. Are not vouchings to warranty[225] beneficial? Those aids of those to whom belongs the reversion of lands brought into plea, and who have the evidence thereof. Also aids of coparceners,[226] who restore *pro rata* if one of them be evicted from the allotted tenement? And yet all these are delays, as, Prince, you well know from my instruction at other times. Such delays other laws do not admit; and the laws of England do not permit frivolous and unfruitful delays. And if less proper delays in pleas have

---

[224] 'Essoins' were excuses sent by defendants for failure to appear. It was possible to secure long delays by appearing and sending essoins alternately, see Plucknett, *Concise History*, 384–5.

[225] Vouchings to warranty were frequently misused for purposes of fraud or delay, see Plucknett, *Concise History*, 411–12.

[226] Aids of coparceners, also sometimes called aid-prayers, were petitions in court to call in the help of another person with an interest in the case, see Plucknett, *Concise History*, 411.

occurred in this realm, they can be cut down in every parliament, and all other laws in use in the realm, if they are defective in any respect, can be amended in every parliament. So it can be rightly concluded that all the laws of this realm are the best in fact or potentiality, since they can easily be brought to it in fact and actual reality.[227] And to do this as often as equity requires it, every king is bound by his oath solemnly taken at the time of his receiving the crown.'[228]

Chapter LIV
The laws of England are the best, which it is expedient for kings to know, yet it suffices for them to know these in general terms

The Prince: 'I fully understand, Chancellor, from your exposition in this dialogue that these laws are not only good but the best. And if some of them need improvement, the rules of parliament teach us that it can quickly be done there.

Hence that realm is always really or potentially governed by the most excellent laws, and I surmise that your teaching in this discourse will not be useless to future kings of England, since they cannot enjoy ruling by laws which they do not appreciate. For the ineptitude of a tool disgusts the artisan, and the weakness of a lance or sword renders the soldier indolent. But as the soldier is stimulated to fight, when not only his weapons are fit but also when he himself is expert in military exercises, so, according to Vegetius, *On Military Matters*, knowledge of war nurtures courage in combat, for no one fears to do what he is confident he has learnt well.[229] Thus every king is stimulated to justice when he knows not only

---

[227] Fortescue is reminding the reader that there exists a mechanism whereby delays and other problems can be resolved; it is possible to actualise potential through parliament. The terms *potentia* and *actus* are Aquinas' translations of the Aristotelian *dynamis* and *energeia*, which are concerned with a theory of action and relate to issues of causation. Every living creature (in this case the body politic) has a composition of potentiality (essence) and actuality (existence) and it constantly strives to actualise its potential, see S. Waterlow, *Nature, Change and Agency in Aristotle's Physics* (Oxford, 1982), 108–21.

[228] See Schramm, *History of the Coronation*, 205–7.

[229] This is also referred to three times in Aquinas, *On Princely Government* and is in Vincent of Beauvais, *On the Moral Education of a Prince*, fo. 105.

that the laws with which he does it are most just, but also that he himself is expert in their form and nature, which it suffices for a prince to know broadly or in general terms, leaving to his judges the detailed and definitive skill and knowledge of the higher branches.

So in the same way, "Every prince ought to have knowledge of the holy scripture", as Vincent of Beauvais says in his book *Of the Moral Education of Princes*,[230] since the scripture above remembered says that "Vain are all in whom is no knowledge of God."[231] And in Proverbs, chapter xvi, it is written, "Let divinity", that is divine judgement or divine speech, "be on the lips of the king", and then, "His mouth shall not err in judgement".[232] Yet a prince is not required to understand the holy scriptures profoundly or definitively, as becomes a professor of sacred theology. For it suffices him to be acquainted in general with its rulings, as in his knowledge of law. Thus did Charles the Great, Louis his son, and Robert, once King of France, who wrote this sequence, "The grace of the Holy Spirit be with us";[233] and many others, as Vincent clearly teaches in the fifteenth chapter of the said book.[234] Hence doctors of law say that, "The Emperor bears all the laws in the casket of his bosom";[235] not because he knows all the laws in reality and in fact, but since he apprehends their principles, and their form and nature likewise, he can be deemed to know all the laws, which he can also transform, change, and abrogate; so that all laws are in him potentially, as Eve was in Adam before she was formed.[236]

But since, Chancellor, you have now persuaded me sufficiently to the study of the laws of England, as you promised to do in the beginning of this work, I will try to solicit you no more on this subject. But I strongly desire you to instruct me in the principles of this law, as you once began, teaching me to know something of its form and nature, because to me this law will always be

---

[230] Vincent of Beauvais, *On the Moral Education of a Prince*, 105v.

[231] Wisdom 13:1 (Vulgate).

[232] Proverbs 16:10.

[233] The full text of this hymn, now thought to have been written by Notkerus Balbulus and not Robert II, is printed in J.P. Migne, *Patrologia Cursus Completus*, CXXI, Series Latina (Paris, 1857–66), 1012.

[234] Vincent of Beauvais, *On the Moral Education of a Prince*, ch.15.

[235] This is *CIC, Code* 6.23.19. See E.H. Kantorowicz, *The King's Two Bodies*, 153–4.

[236] The comparison is with parliament, that is, with the realm as a body and with the serjeants and justices.

exceptional among all other laws of the earth, among which I see it shine like Venus among the stars. And since I do not doubt that intention of yours, which moved you to this discourse, is now satisfied, time and reason demand that we bring our discussion to an end, giving thanks and praise to Him who began, continued, and finished it, whom we call Alpha and Omega,[237] and whom let every spirit praise. Amen.'

[237] Revelation 1:8.

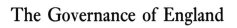

The Governance of England

The Governance of England

Chapter 1
The difference between 'royal dominion' and 'political and royal dominion'

There are two kinds of kingdoms, one of which is a lordship called in Latin *dominium regale*, and the other is called *dominium politicum et regale*.[1] And they differ in that the first king may rule his people by such laws as he makes himself and therefore he may set upon them taxes and other impositions, such as he wills himself, without their assent. The second king may not rule his people by other laws than such as they assent to and therefore he may set upon them no impositions without their own assent.

This diversity is well taught by Saint Thomas, in his book which he wrote to the king of Cyprus *On Princely Government*.[2] But yet it is more clearly treated in a book called *Compendium of Moral Philosophy*,[3] and somewhat also by Giles in his book *On Princely*

---

[1] Cf. *In Praise of the Laws of England*, chs, IX-XIII and Appendix A. For discussion of the meaning of these terms, see Introduction and articles by Gilbert, 'Fortescue's "dominium regale et politicum"' and Burns 'Fortescue and the Political Theory of *dominium*'.

[2] Aquinas, *On Princely Government*. Only the first book and the first four chapters of the second book are now thought to have been written by Aquinas; it was continued by Ptolemy of Lucca. References to the later sections are to pseudo-Aquinas. For editions, see 'Select bibliography'.

[3] Roger of Waltham (*floruit c.* 1300). His *Compendium Morale* (Bodleian Laud MS Misc. 616) is a series of moral disputations on the virtues and duties of a prince.

Government.[4] The children of Israel, as Saint Thomas says,[5] after God had chosen them as 'his own people and holy realm',[6] were ruled by Him under Judges 'royally and politically', until the time that they desired to have a king such as all the gentiles, which we call pagans, then had, but they had no king but rather a man who reigned upon them 'only royally'. With which desire God was greatly offended, as well for their folly, as for their unkindness since they had a king, which was God, who reigned upon them politically and royally, and yet they would change him for a king, a man who would reign upon them only royally.

And therefore God, threatening them, made them afraid by thunders and other terrifying things from the heavens. And when they would not thereby leave their foolish desire, he charged the prophet Samuel to declare to them the law of such a king as they asked; who, among other things, said that he would take from them their land and give it to his servants, and set their children in his carts, and do to them many such other harmful things, as appears in the eighth chapter of the first Book of Kings.[7] Whereas before that time, while they were ruled by God royally and politically under Judges, it was not lawful for any man to take from them any of their goods, or to injure their children who had not offended.

Whereby it may appear that in those days 'political and royal government' was distinguished 'from only royal government' and that it was better for the people to be ruled politically and royally, than to be ruled only royally. Saint Thomas also in his said book praises 'political and royal dominion', because the prince who reigns by such lordship may not freely fall into tyranny, as may the prince who reigns 'only royally'.[8] And yet they are both equal in estate and in power, as may easily be shown and proved by infallible reason.[9]

---

[4] Giles of Rome (*c.* 1243–1316), also referred to as Aegidius Romanus and Egidio Colonna, was a pupil of Aquinas at Paris 1269–1272, he wrote his *On Princely Government* for Philip IV. Reference is to III.ii.

[5] Pseudo-Aquinas, *De Regimine Principum*, II.viii and ix.

[6] This a combination of Deuteronomy 14:2 and Exodus 19:6.

[7] I Samuel 8:10–18. Aquinas, *Summa Theologica* Ia IIae qu. 4 art. 1; pseudo-Aquinas, *De Regimine Principum*, II.ix and III.xi.

[8] Aquinas, *On Princely Government* I.vi and see Burns 'Fortescue and the Political Theory of *dominium*'.

[9] Cf. *In Praise of the Laws of England*, chs. XI, XIV, XXXIV and XXXVII and *On the Nature of the Law of Nature*, Appendix A.

Chapter 2
Why one king reigns 'royally', and another 'politically and royally'

Some men may perhaps wonder why one realm is a lordship only royal, and the prince thereof rules it by his law called 'royal law', and another kingdom is a lordship royal and political, and the prince thereof rules it by a law called 'political and royal law',[10] since these two princes are of equal estate. This doubt may be answered in this way.

The first institution of these two realms upon the incorporation of them is the cause of this diversity.[11] When Nimrod, by might for his own glory, made and incorporated the first realm and subdued it to himself by tyranny, he would not have it governed by any other rule or law, but by his own will, by which and for the accomplishment thereof he made it. And therefore though he had thus made himself a realm, holy scripture disdained to call him a king, 'since *rex* is so called from *regendo* or ruling',[12] which thing he did not, but oppressed the people by force, and therefore he was a tyrant and called 'the first of the tyrants'. But holy writ calls him 'a mighty hunter before the Lord'. For as the hunter takes the wild beast in order to slay and eat him, so Nimrod subdued to him the people by force, in order to have their service and their goods, exercising over them the lordship that is called 'only royal dominion'.[13]

After him Belus who was first called a king, after him his son Ninus, and after him other pagans, who by example of Nimrod made themselves realms, would not have them ruled by other laws

---

[10] The Latin here is 'Ius regale', and 'Ius politicum et regale'. Fortescue explains the difference between 'ius' and 'lex' in *On the Nature of the Law of Nature* I.xxx. Deriving 'ius' from 'iustitia', that is, that which is 'bona et aequa', he says that 'lex' is a species of 'ius' which constrains or binds – 'lex' as 'vinculum iuris'. He also states that 'lex' or 'ius' can be used with reference to jurisdiction, but that only 'ius' is used to refer to a title to possession.

[11] Cf. *In Praise of the Laws of England*, ch.XIII.

[12] For 'rex a regendo', see Augustine, *City of God* V.xii and Isidore of Seville, *Etymologies*, IX.3 and *In Praise of the Laws of Nature*, n. 68.

[13] The example of Nimrod is from Genesis 10:8–12. See Augustine, *City of God*, XVI.iii, Isidore of Seville, *Etymologies* VII.6 and John of Salisbury, *Policraticus*, VIII.20. Fortescue possibly used his own copy of Vincent of Beauvais *On the Moral Education of a Prince* for the reference, Bodleian Rawlinson MS C 298. Nimrod is extensively used as the 'first tyrant' whose rule was founded by conquest.

than by their own wills.[14] Which laws are very good under good princes, and their kingdoms then most resemble the kingdom of God, who reigns upon man ruling him by His own will. Wherefore many Christian princes use the same law, and therefore it is that the laws say, 'what pleased the prince has the force of law'.[15] And thus I suppose 'only royal dominion' first began in realms.

But afterwards, when mankind was more civilised,[16] and better disposed to virtue, [there arose] great communities, as was the fellowship that came in to this land with Brutus,[17] willing to be united and made a body politic called a realm, having a head to govern it – since, following the saying of the Philosopher, every community united of many parts must needs have a head[18] – then they chose the same Brutus to be their head and king. And they and he upon this incorporation, institution, and uniting of themselves into a realm, ordained the same realm to be ruled and governed by such laws as they would all assent to, which law is therefore called 'political', and, because it is administered by a king, it is called 'royal'.[19]

'*Policia* is so called from *poles*, that is many, and *ycos*, that is, wisdom; by which political government is called government administered by the wisdom and counsel of many.'[20] The king of

---

[14] For Belus and Ninus, see Augustine, *City of God*, IV.vi, XVI.iii and xvii, XVIII.ii. Cf. *On the Nature of the Law of Nature*, I.viii.

[15] 'Quod principi placuit legis habet vigorem' is the Roman law *lex regia*, *CIC Institutes* I.2.6 and CIC Digest I.4.1. Cf. *In Praise of the Laws of England*, chs. IX and XXXIV, 17 and 48.

[16] The original word here is 'mansuete' which means 'tame', 'gentle' or 'mild'. Consent as the basis for power is clearly portrayed as a more advanced form of government. In *On the Nature of the Law of Nature* I.xvi, Fortescue describes Octavian, who ruled 'royally and politically', as 'mansuetissimus', see Appendix A, 129.

[17] Brutus, great grandson of Aeneas, was the founder of Britain according to Geoffrey of Monmouth's *History of the Kings of Britain*. Fortescue probably took his reference, however, from Richard Rede's 'Chronicle' (of which he owned a copy, Bodleian Rawlinson MS C 398) or from Vincent of Beauvais, *On the Moral Education of a Prince*, ch.2, Bodleian Rawlinson MS C 398, fo. 91r.

[18] Taken from pseudo-Aquinas, *De Regimine Principum*, III.9. Cf *In Praise of the Laws of England*, ch. III.

[19] In this account of the incorporation of the realm, Fortescue appears to envisage two distinct acts – a compact and then the election of a head. In the corresponding passage of *In Praise of the Laws of England* (ch. XIII, 20) the formation of the realm as a body politic complete with a head seems to happen 'all in one go'.

[20] Origin unknown, but Ptolemy of Lucca (pseudo-Aquinas) also derived 'politicum' from 'plurium', *De Regimine Principum* IV.i. Cf. *On the Nature of the Law of Nature* I.xxiii.

the Scots reigns upon his people by this law, that is to say, 'by political and royal government'.[21] And, as Diodorus Siculus says in his book *Ancient Histories*, the realm of Egypt is ruled by the same law,[22] and therefore the king thereof does not change his laws without the assent of his people. And, as he says, the kingdom of Saba in Arabia Felix is ruled in like form,[23] and the land of Libya[24] and also the majority of all the realms of Africa.[25] Which manner of rule and lordship the said Diodorus in that book praises greatly; for it is not only good for the prince, who may thereby the more surely do justice than by his own arbitrament; but it is also good for his people who receive thereby such justice as they desire themselves.

Now, as it seems to me, it is shown clearly enough, why one king reigns upon his people 'by only royal dominion', and the other reigns 'by political and royal dominion'; for the former kingdom began of and by the might of the prince, and the latter began by the desire and institution of the people of the same prince.

Chapter 3
Here are shown the fruits of 'royal law' and the fruits of 'political and royal law'[26]

And although the French king reigns upon his people 'by royal dominion',[27] yet neither Saint Louis, sometime king there, nor any of his progenitors, ever set any taxes or other imposition upon the people of that land without the assent of the three estates,[28] which

[21] See A. Grant, *Independence and Nationhood: Scotland 1306–1469*, 166–70 and J.D. Mackie, *A History of Scotland* (2nd edn, London, 1978), chs. 5 and 6.

[22] Diodorus Siculus, *Library of History, Ancient Histories*, I.69.

[23] Diodorus Siculus, *Library of History, Ancient Histories*, III.49.

[24] Diodorus Siculus, *Library of History, Ancient Histories*, III.46–47.

[25] Diodorus Siculus, *Library of History, Ancient Histories*, III.5. Cf. *In Praise of the Laws of England*, ch. XIII, 22 for Ethiopia.

[26] This chapter is to be compared with *In Praise of the Laws of England*, Chs. XXXV and XXXVI, 49–51 and 51–3.

[27] Cf. the French jurist Philippe de Remi, sire de Beaumanoir (*c.* 1250–1296)): 'qui lui plaît à faire, doit être tenu pour loi', cited by Plummer, *The Governance of England*, 193. For a comparison of Beaumanoir's *Coutumes de Beauvaisis* with Bracton and Glanville, see J. Dunbabin in J.H. Burns (ed.) *Cambridge History of Medieval Political Thought*, esp. 486.

[28] St Louis was King Louis IX of France (1226–1270). On the estates general, see P.S. Lewis, 'The Failure of the French Medieval Estates' in P.S. Lewis (ed.), trans. G.F. Martin, *The Recovery of France in the Fifteenth Century*, ch. 10, 294–311.

when they are assembled are like the court of the parliament in England.[29] And many of his successors kept this order until recently, when Englishmen made such war in France, that the three estates dared not come together. And then for that reason and for the great necessity of goods which the French king had for the defence of that land, he took it upon himself to set taxes and other impositions upon the commons without the assent of the three estates.[30] But yet he would not, nor has, set any such charges upon the nobles, for fear of rebellion.[31] And because the commons there, though they have grumbled, have not rebelled or dared to rebel, the French kings have every year since set such charges upon them, and have so augmented the same charges, that the same commons are so impoverished and destroyed, that they can barely live.[32]

[29] Cf. Philippe de Commynes, 'this type of preparation [for war] takes a long time there [in England] because the king cannot undertake such an exploit without assembling his Parliament, the equivalent of our Three Estates, which is a very just and laudable institution, and on account of this the kings are stronger and better served when they consult parliament in such matters. When these Estates are assembled, the king declares his intentions and asks for aid from his subjects, because he cannot raise any taxes in England, except for an expedition to France or Scotland or some other such comparable cause. They will grant them, very willingly and liberally, especially for crossing to France. There is a well-known trick which these kings of England practise when they want to amass money. They pretend to want to attack Scotland and to assemble armies. To raise a large sum of money they pay them for three months and then disband their army and return home, although they have received money for a year. King Edward understood this ruse perfectly and he often did this', *Memoirs The Reign of Louis XI 1461–1483*, IV.2, 225.

[30] A standing army and permanent *taille* were established in 1439, see further, J.H. Shennan, *Government and Society in France 1461–1661*, 35–7.

[31] The military service owed by the nobility exempted them from taxation, see Shennan, *Government and Society*, 25–8.

[32] Cf. 'At the time I am speaking about, everybody, whether of high, middle or low rank, thought the kingdom very expensive to run because they had borne and suffered for twenty years and more appalling taxes . . . Certainly it was pitiful to see and learn about the poverty of the people but our master had one good quality; he never amassed a fortune. He took everything and spent everything . . . In some respects it would have been better if he had done less, because he took from the poor to give to those who had no need of it', Commynes, *Memoirs*, V.19, 346. Also, 'King Charles VII, at the time of his death used to raise in all 1,800,000 francs from his kingdom. His soldiers consisted of about 1,700 men-at-arms in the ordinance companies who maintained order by guarding the provinces of the kingdom, yet for a long time before his death they had not ridden around the country, which was a great relief to the people. At the time of our master's death he was receiving 4,700,000 francs and he had some four to five thousand men-at-arms and more than 25,000 infantry', *Memoirs* VI.6, 388. See also, P-R. Gaussin, *Louis XI: Roi Méconnu*, Book II, ch. II, 150–96.

They drink water, they eat apples with very brown bread made of rye, they eat no meat other than very seldom a little bacon, or the entrails and heads of beasts slain for the nobles and merchants of the land. They wear no wool, unless a poor coat under their outermost garment which is made of great canvas and is called a frock. Their hose are of the same canvas, and do not pass their knees, wherefore they are gartered and their thighs bare. Their wives and children go barefoot. They can live no other way. For those who were accustomed to pay their lord one scute for a tenement, hired by the year, now pay the king five more scutes over and above that one. Wherefore they are compelled by necessity continually to look out for labour and grub in the ground for their sustenance, such that their nature is wasted, and their kin are brought to nought. They walk crookedly and are feeble, not able to fight, nor to defend the realm; nor have they weapons, nor money with which to buy themselves weapons. But truly they live in the most extreme poverty and misery, and yet they dwell in one of the most fertile realms of the world.

Wherefore the French king has no men of his own realm able to defend it, except his nobles, who do not bear such impositions, and are therefore very physically able; for which reason the said king is compelled to make his armies and retinues for the defence of his land of foreigners,[33] such as Scots,[34] Spaniards, Aragonese, men of Germany[35] and of other nations; or else all his enemies might overrun him; for he has no defence of his own except his castles and fortresses. Lo this is the fruit of his 'royal law'.

If the realm of England, which is an island and therefore may not easily get succour of other lands, were ruled under such a law, and under such a prince, it would then be a prey to all other nations who wanted to conquer, rob, or devour it; which was well proved in the time of the Britons, when the Scots and the Picts so beat and oppressed this land, that the people thereof sought help of the Romans, to whom they had been tributary. And when they could not be defended by them, they sought help of the duke of Brittany,

---

[33] Cf. Giles of Rome, *On Princely Government*, III.ii.6 where he states that the use of foreigners, as opposed to citizens, as protection, is the mark of a tyrant.

[34] For a reference to Louis XI's Scots Guard, see Commynes, *Memoirs*, II.12, 157.

[35] This is probably a reference to the Swiss, see Shennan, *Government and Society*, 36 and Gaussin, *Louis XI*, 263–9 and 326–33.

then called little Brittany, and granted therefore to make his brother Constantine their king.[36] And so he was made king here, and reigned many years, and his children after him, of which the great Arthur was one of their issue.[37]

But, blessed be God, this land is ruled under a better law; and therefore the people thereof are not in such penury, nor thereby hurt in their persons, but they are wealthy, and have all things necessary to the sustenance of nature. Wherefore they are mighty, and able to resist the adversaries of this realm, and to beat other realms that do, or want to do, them wrong. Lo this is the fruit of 'political and royal law', under which we live. Now I have somewhat shown the fruits of both laws, 'so that by their fruits you shall know them'.[38]

Chapter 4
Here is shown how the revenues of France have been made great

Since our king reigns upon us by laws more favourable and good to us, than are the laws by which the French king rules his people, it stands to reason that we should do more good and be more profitable to him than the subjects of the French king are to him; which it would seem that we are not, considering that his subjects yield to him more in a year, than we do to our sovereign lord in two years, although they do so against their wills.

Nevertheless when it is considered, a king's office stands in two things: one, to defend his realm against their external enemies by the sword, the other, that he defend his people against internal wrongdoers by justice, as it appears by the said first Book of Kings.[39]

---

[36] See Geoffrey of Monmouth, *History of the Kings of Britain* VI.1–5, 144–51. An account is also in Rede's 'Chronicle', Bodleian Rawlinson MS C 398, fos 11–12.

[37] See Geoffrey of Monmouth, *History of the Kings of Britain* VIII.19–20, 204–8.

[38] The full reference is 'Beware of false prophets, who come to you in sheep's clothing but inwardly are ravenous wolves. You will know them by their fruits. Are grapes gathered from thorns or figs from thistles? So, every sound tree bears good fruit, but the bad tree bears evil fruit. A sound tree cannot bear evil fruit, nor can a bad tree bear good fruit. Every tree that does not bear good fruit is cut down and thrown into the fire. Thus you will know them by their fruits', Matthew 7:15–20. Cf. *In Praise of the Laws of England*, ch. XLII, 60.

[39] I Samuel 8:20. In 1454 when York was made Protector, it was said that this 'imports a personal duty of attendance to the actual defence of this land, as well against enemies outward, if case require, as against rebels inward, if any happen to be', *Rot. Parl.*, V.242. In the parliamentary sermon of 1467, bishop Stillington

This the French king does not, though he keeps justice between subject and subject; since he oppresses them more himself, than would have done all the wrongdoers of the realm, though they had no king. And since it is a sin to give no meat, drink, clothing or other alms to those who have need, as shall be declared at the Day of Judgement, how much greater a sin is it to take from the poor man his meat, his drink, his clothing, and all that he has need of? Which truly the French king does to many thousands of his subjects, as is before clearly declared.

Which thing though it is now disguised 'as royal law', yet it is tyranny. For, as Saint Thomas says, when a king rules his realm only to his own profit, and not to the good of his subjects, he is a tyrant.[40] King Herod reigned upon the Jews 'by royal dominion'; yet when he slew the children of Israel, he was in that a tyrant,[41] even though the laws say, 'what pleased the prince has the force of law'.[42] Wherefore Ahab who reigned upon the children of Israel by like law, and desired to have Naboth his subject's vineyard, would not by that law take it from him, but proferred him the value thereof.[43] For these words said to the prophet, 'declare to them the royal law',[44] is not to say otherwise than, 'declare to them the power of the king'.

Wherefore as often as such a king does anything against the law of God, or against the law of nature, he does wrong, notwithstanding the said law declared by the prophet. And it is so, what the law of nature wills in this case, that the king should do to his subjects, as he would be done to himself,[45] if he were a subject;[46] which would not be that he would be almost destroyed as are the commons of

said of the king that 'his final intent was to minister law and justice, and to plant, fix and set peace through all this his realm . . . and also intended to provide an outward peace for the defence and safety of this realm', *Rot. Parl.* v.622.

[40] Aquinas, *On Princely Government*, I.i, from Aristotle, *Politics*, III.vii.

[41] Matthew 2:16–18. Cf. *On the Nature of the Law of Nature* I.xxviii.

[42] *Institutes* I.2.6 and *Digest* I.4.1. Cf. *The Governance*, ch.2, 86 and *In Praise of the Laws of England*, chs. IX and XXXIV, 17 and 48.

[43] I Kings 22 and in pseudo-Aquinas, *De Regimine Principum* III.xi.

[44] I Samuel 8:9.

[45] The 'Golden Rule' or 'law of the prophets' of doing to others as you would be done to, is to be found in Matthew 7:12 and in Gratian's *Decretum, distinctio 1,* in A. Friedberg (ed.), *Corpus Iuris Canonici pars prior: Decretum Magistri Gratiani.* In *On the Nature of the Law of Nature* I.iv, Fortescue explains that it is to be considered as part of the law of Nature. The argument is largely derived from Aquinas, *Summa Theologica* Ia IIae qus. 90–108, esp. 94–5.

[46] Cf. *In Praise of the Laws of England*, ch. XXVII 41.

France. Wherefore, albeit that the French king's revenues are by such means much greater than are the revenues which the king our sovereign lord has of us, yet they are not rightly taken, and the might of his land is almost destroyed thereby.

By which consideration I do not want the king's revenues of this realm to be made great by any such means. And yet of necessity they must be greater than they are at present. And truly it is very necessary that they are always great, and that the king should have abundantly the means by which his estate may be honourably kept for very many reasons, of which some shall now be remembered.

Chapter 5
The harm that comes of a king's poverty

First, if a king is poor, he shall by necessity make his expenses, and buy all that is necessary to his estate, by credit and borrowing; wherefore his creditors will win upon him the fourth or the fifth penny of all that he spends. And so he shall lose, when he pays, the fourth or the fifth penny of his revenues, and thus be thereby ever poorer and poorer, as usury and chevisance increases the poverty of he who borrows.[47] His creditors shall always grumble for lack of their payment, and defame his highness of misgovernance, and default of keeping of payment days; which if he keeps, he must borrow as much at the payment days, as he did first; for he shall then be poorer than he was by the value of the fourth or fifth part of his first expenses, and so be ever poorer and poorer, until the time when he is the poorest lord of his land. For such manner of borrowing makes the great lords to be poorer than their tenants.

What dishonour this is, and abating of the glory of a king.[48] But yet it is most to his insecurity. For his subjects will rather go with a lord who is rich, and may pay their wages and expenses, than with their king who has nothing in his purse, such that they must serve him, if they want to do so, at their own expense.

Likewise, if the king is poor, he shall of necessity make his gifts and rewards by assignments, for which he shall have but little

[47] See K.B. MacFarlane, 'Loans to the Lancastrian kings', *Cambridge Historical Journal* 9 (1947), 51–68 and G.L. Harriss, 'Aids, loans and benevolences', *HJ* 6 (1963).
[48] Cf. Aquinas, *On Princely Government*, I.vii.

thanks. For the poor man would rather have a hundred marks in hand, than a hundred pounds by assignment, which perhaps shall cost him very much before he can get his payment, and perhaps never be paid thereof.[49] And often for lack of money the king shall be glad to give away his land to such as would have preferred a hundred pounds in hand, than of land worth £40 yearly, to the great abating of his revenues and depopulation of his realm.[50]

But the greatest harm that comes of a king's poverty is that he shall by necessity be compelled to find extreme means of getting goods; such as to accuse some of his subjects who are innocent, and upon the rich men more than the poor, so that he may better pay; and to show rigour where favour ought to be shown, and favour where rigour should be shown, to perversion of justice, and perturbation of the peace and quiet of the realm.[51] For, as the Philosopher says in his *Ethics*, 'It is impossible to do good works without resources'.[52]

It is not now necessary to specify more of the harms which come to a realm by the poverty of their king, although there are many more than we have shown yet, for every wise man may see them clearly enough. But we must hold it to be undoubted, that no realm may prosper, nor be worshipful, under a poor king.

---

[49] Most of the Crown's creditors received payment in the form of assignments rather than cash. These assignments were promises of repayment at a future date in the form of drafts in anticipation of revenue being collected by, for example, sheriffs or customs collectors. Increasingly, however, the revenue was 'spent', and the tallies of assignment failed to be met. See A.L. Brown, *The Governance of Late Medieval England 1272–1461* (London, 1989) 80–84 and E.F. Jacob *The Fifteenth Century 1399–1485*, 436–9.

[50] The manifesto of the Yorkist lords in 1460 complains of 'the poverty and misery that . . . our sovereign lord stands in, not having any livelihood of the crown of England whereof he may keep his honourable household, which causes the spilling of his liegemen', *English Chronicle*, 86.

[51] These 'extreme means' would include benevolences and the rigorous enforcement of penal statutes, see E.F. Jacob, *The Fifteenth Century 1399–1485*, 436–46 and, for future developments, see Goodman, *The New Monarchy*.

[52] This is *Auctoritates Aristotelis*, 234, from Aristotle, *Ethics*, I.viii.15.

Chapter 6
Ordinance for the king's ordinary charges[53]

And since it is necessary for the king always to be rich, which may not happen unless he has revenues sufficient for the yearly maintenance of his estate, it is useful that we first estimate what his yearly charges and expenses are likely to amount to because his revenues need to be proportioned according to that.[54] But yet they need to be greater than will be the charges, for fear of sudden occurrences, which may happen to him and to his realm. For Saint Bernard says that if a man's expenses are equal to his livelihood, a sudden chance may destroy his estate.[55]

The king's yearly expenses consist in ordinary charges and in extraordinary charges. His ordinary charges may not be eschewed, and therefore livelihood needs to be assigned for the payment thereof, which livelihood is to be put to no other use.[56] And if it happens that any patent is made of any part thereof to other use, then that patent shall be void and of no effect. If this is firmly established, the king's ordinary charges may always be paid in hand, and the provision for them may always be made at the proper time, which shall be worth to the king the fourth or the fifth part of the quantity of his expenses for ordinary charges.

[53] See Myers, *The Household of Edward IV* and Mertes, *The English Noble Household.*

[54] Edward IV told the assembled parliament in 1467: 'the cause why I have called and summoned this my present parliament is that I purpose to live upon mine own and not to charge my subjects except in great and urgent causes, concerning more the weal of themselves, and also the defence of them and of this my realm, rather than mine own', *Rot. Parl.* v.572.

[55] St Bernard (attributed to), *Epistola De Cura Rei Familiaris*, IV, ed. J.R. Lumby (EETS, London, 1870) 229.

[56] On the ordinary charges, cf. Appendix C, 4–5, 141–2. Plummer edn 216–17 cites Robert Redesdale's petition of 1469: 'We, the King's true and faithful Commons and subjects of this land, meekly beseech . . . that it will please him [Edward IV] for the great weal of himself, his heirs and the commonweal of us his true subjects and Commons . . . to establish for ever to be had such a sufficiency of livelihood and possessions, by the which he and all his heirs after him may maintain and keep their most honourable estate, with all other ordinary charges necessary to be had in this land. So that neither he nor any of his heirs hereafter, need of necessity to charge and lay upon his true Commons and subjects such great impositions as before is expressed; unless it were for the great and urgent causes concerning as well the weal of us as of our said sovereign lord.'

This in no way restrains the king's power. For it is no power to be able to alienate and put away; but it is a power to be able to have and keep to himself. Just as it is no power to be able to sin, and to do ill, or to be able to be sick, or to grow old, or for a man to be able to hurt himself. For all these powers come of impotency. And therefore they may properly be called non-powers. Wherefore the holy spirits and angels, who are not able to sin, grow old, be sick, or hurt themselves have more power than we, who may harm ourselves with all these defects.[57] So the king's power is greater, in that he may not put from himself possessions necessary for his own sustenance, than if he might put them from himself, and alienate the same to his own hurt and harm.

Nor is this against the king's prerogative, by which he is exalted above his subjects, but rather this is to him a prerogative. For no man save he may have again the land that he has once alienated. This livelihood assigned for the ordinary charges shall never afterwards be asked of the king, nor shall his highness think therefore that he has greater livelihood to be given away. And so by reason hereof he will the more restrain his gifts of the rest of his livelihood, considering that then it will not be great, and therefore he shall have more need of it than shall those who will ask for it.

The ordinary charges, which this writer can now remember, are these: the king's household and his wardrobe.[58] And although the king wishes now, or will hereafter, to make his household less than it used to be; yet his highness shall then have therefore about his person, for his honour and safety, lords, knights, and squires, and others, in as great a number, or greater, than his household used to be, for charges perhaps as great as his household well-ruled used to stand him in. Wherefore herein it is not necessary to consider or to purvey, except only for the king's house, which he may resume or change into his new fashion, or other form at his pleasure, and as it shall be thought most expedient according to the seasons. The expenses of which household may soon be estimated by those who have been officers therein, and by the clerks of the exchequer.

[57] The idea of 'non-power' or 'impotence' is crucial to Fortescue's theory. Cf. Appendix A, 133 and *In Praise of the Laws of England*, ch. xiv, 24 and see Introduction, xxix.

[58] For the household and wardrobe, see Myers, *The Household of Edward IV*.

The second ordinary charge is the payment of the wages and fees of the king's great officers, his courts and his counsel.[59] Which charge will always be great, and these men need always to be promptly paid. For poverty in them is not only unworshipful, but it may do the most harm that may come of any need in any estate of the land, after the king's most great estate.

The third ordinary charge is the payment of the keeping of the marches,[60] wherein we bear much greater charges yearly than do the Scots, which is often because of the favour that we do to the persons who keep them, which favour the Scots do not.

The fourth charge is the keeping of Calais, which charge is well enough known.

The fifth charge is for the king's works, of which the yearly expenses may not be estimated, but yet the accounts of the clerks of the works will give an idea of them, for as long as the king makes no new works.[61]

The keeping of the sea I do not count among the ordinary charges because, although the charge thereof is borne yearly, it is not estimable, and the king has for that purpose the subsidy of poundage and tonnage. Nevertheless poundage and tonnage cannot therefore be reckoned as part of the revenues which the king has for the maintenance of his estate, because it ought to be applied only to the keeping of the sea.[62]

And though we are not always at war upon the sea, yet it is necessary that the king always has some fleet, for the repressing of pirates[63] to protect our merchants, our fishers,[64] and the dwellers

---

[59] On wages and fees, see Myers, *The Household of Edward IV*. In the MS Digby 145 written by Sir Adrian Fortescue there is inserted here 'his Garde and other servants'. Edward IV set up his own personal guard in 1467.

[60] These were the east and west Marches of Scotland. In 1461 Warwick had been appointed sole warden of the Marches. In 1463, the east March was given to Warwick's brother Montague, and in 1470, Richard duke of Gloucester was appointed warden of the west March.

[61] See Myers, *The Household of Edward IV*.

[62] Grants of tunnage and poundage were granted for life to Henry V (1415), Henry VI (1453) and Edward IV (1463). The revenue was supposed to be reserved for the 'keeping of the sea' but was diverted for various purposes, see, for example, the complaint against Suffolk, *Rot. Parl.*, V. 180.

[63] In 26 Henry VI several enquiries into piracy were ordered, *Calendar Patent Rolls*, vol. V, Henry VI. See *Rot. Parl.* VI. 138 for the activities of the Cornish pirate, Henry Bodrugan.

[64] See *PL* III. 81 (1473).

upon our coasts,[65] and also that the king always keeps some great and mighty vessels, for the defeat of an army when any shall be made against him upon the sea. For then it shall be too late to have such vessels made. And yet without them, all the king's navy shall not suffice to assail carracks and other great vessels, nor yet to be able to break up a mighty fleet gathered purposely.[66]

Now, as I suppose, we have reckoned the greatest part of the king's ordinary charges. Wherefore we will consider next his extraordinary charges, as far as may be possible to us.

Chapter 7
The king's extraordinary charges

The king's extraordinary charges are so irregular, that no man may know them in certainty, but yet he may estimate what sum they are not likely to exceed, unless there happens an excessively exorbitant case. And then it shall be reasonable, and also necessary, that all the realm bear for that case a special charge. Such of the said extraordinary charges as this writer can now remember are these.

First, the king shall often send out of this land his ambassadors,[67] as well to the pope as to divers kings, princes and nations. And at other times he shall send his procurators and messengers to the general councils.[68] Which ambassadors, procurators and messengers shall need to be honourably accompanied and highly regarded, as much for the worship of the realm, as for the advancing of the matters for which they shall be sent. And this is to the king's very great charge, which shall be more or less, after their long or short stay in their voyage.

Likewise, the king shall bear unknown yearly charges in receiving of legates and messengers sent from the pope, and ambassadors sent from kings and other princes, and also from great communities

---

[65] In 1442 there were complaints that it was not safe on the coasts, *Rot.Parl.*, V. 52.

[66] A list of the fleet under Henry V (1417) gives twenty-four, *PPC*, ii. 202. The depletion of the fleet under Henry VI caused much adverse comment, see, for example, *The Libelle of English Polycye*, II, 159 (in Jacob, *The Fifteenth Century*, 346–9) where it is said that England's enemies suggest that a sheep should supplant the ship on the coinage.

[67] Plummer edn, 241–2 gives details of the wages of ambassadors.

[68] Ambassadors were sent to the councils of Pisa (1409), Constance (1414), Pavia (1423), Basle (1431) and Ferrara (1438).

beyond the sea, which will put the king to great expenses while they are here, and at their departing they must needs have great gifts and rewards. For that befits the king's magnificence and liberality and it is also necessary for the worship of his realm.

Likewise, since it is not good that he [the king] should reward such as do, or shall do him service, or other manner of pleasures, with the possessions and revenues of his crown, nor with other possessions of his inheritance – for they be much more necessary for the sustenance of his great estate – it shall therefore be necessary, that the king make such rewards with money out of his coffers, and that some of them have so largely thereof, as they may with it buy themselves land, if they want to. For by this mean the king's estate shall always be kept unblemished. And of some men his highness shall have more thanks for money than for land. Also money is the most fitting reward to him who has not long served. This charge will always be great, and so inestimably great, that in some year a great lord's livelihood shall not suffice to bear it, even if he sells a great part thereof. And truly, when the king rewards his servants in this manner, he shows great favour to all his realm.

Likewise, it is necessary that the king has such treasure that he may make new buildings when he wants to, for his pleasure and magnificence, and such that he may buy himself rich clothes and rich furs other than usually fall under the yearly charges of his wardrobe, rich stones, cloth, belts, and other jewels and ornaments convenient to his estate royal.[69] And often he will buy rich hangings and other apparel for his houses; vessels, vestments, and other ornaments for his chapel; he may also buy expensive horses, trappers, and incur such other noble and great costs, as befits his royal majesty, of which it is not now possible for this writer to remember the particulars. For if a king did not do so, nor might not be able to do so, he would live then not like his estate, but rather in misery, and in more subjection than does a private person.

Likewise, the king shall often send his commissioners in great force, and also his judges, to repress and punish rioters and risers.[70]

---

[69] In 1441, Henry VI ordered all of his royal jewels to be coined, sold or pledged for the preservation of the kingdom of France and the Duchy of Normandy, *PPC* V, 132.

[70] Fortescue had himself sat on many commissions of *oyer et terminer*, see Chrimes, *De laudibus*, lix–lxvii.

For which cause he shall at other times ride in his own person accompanied in force.[71] Which thing cannot be done without great costs, for no man is bound to serve him in such cases at his own expense.

Likewise, if there comes a sudden army upon this land by sea or by land, the king must encounter them with a like army, or a greater. For the expenses whereof he shall not so suddenly have any aid of his people. Wherefore he must then meet the expenses with money out of his own coffers, or put his whole land in jeopardy.

Lo, now we have remembered a great part of the king's extraordinary charges; and before we have shown great part of his ordinary charges. Wherefore now it is time to show how the king may have revenues and livelihood sufficient to bear these two charges.

Chapter 8
If the king's livelihood does not suffice, his subjects ought to make it sufficient

It has been shown before, how necessary it is that sufficient livelihood is assigned for the king's ordinary charges, and that the same livelihood is only applied thereto, and not alienated in future. For that assignment may not hurt the king in any way, considering that if any part of the revenues thereof remain over and above the payment of the same ordinary charges, that which remains is the king's own money, which he may then employ to other use at his own pleasure. And it is undoubted that the king has sufficient livelihood which may be so assigned for his ordinary charges.

Wherefore we have now to enquire about nothing more than what livelihood the king has for the payment of his extraordinary charges, over and above the amount of livelihood which shall be assigned for his ordinary charges. And, if he does not have livelihood sufficient thereto, how then his livelihood may be made sufficient.

For his realm is bound by right to sustain him in everything necessary to his estate. For, as Saint Thomas says, 'the king is given for the kingdom, and not the kingdom for the king'.[72] Wherefore

---

[71] Henry VI did so after Cade's rebellion in 1450, see *Three Fifteenth-Century Chronicles*, 68–9.

[72] Pseudo-Aquinas, *De Regimine Principum* III.xi. Cf. *On the Nature of the Law of Nature*, I.xxv and *In Praise of the Laws of England*, ch. xxxvii, 53.

all that he does ought to be referred to his kingdom. For though his estate is the highest temporal estate on earth, yet it is an office, in which he ministers to his realm defence and justice. And therefore he may say of himself and of his realm, as the pope says of himself and of the Church, in that he writes, 'servant of the servants of God'.[73] By which reason, just as every servant ought to have his sustenance of him whom he serves, so ought the pope to be sustained by the Church, and the king by his realm. For 'no-one should serve as a soldier at his own expense'.[74] And our Lord says, 'the labourer deserves his food'.[75] Wherefore the apostle says, 'let him who is taught the word share all good things with him who teaches'.[76] Wherefore since every realm is bound to sustain its king, yet much more are we bound thereto, we, upon whom our king reigns by laws as favourable as is before declared.

Chapter 9
Here he shows the perils that may come to the king by over-mighty subjects

But since the said extraordinary charges are so uncertain that they are not estimable, it is not possible to be certain what annual livelihood will suffice to sustain him. Wherefore we need in this case to use conjecture and imagination to think that there is no lord's livelihood in England sufficient to bear the king's extraordinary charges. Then it is necessary that the king's livelihood, over and above such revenues as shall be assigned for his ordinary charges, are greater than the livelihood of the greatest lord in England.[77]

And perhaps, when livelihood sufficient for the king's ordinary charges is limited and assigned thereto, it shall appear that divers lords of England have as much livelihood of their own, as shall then remain in the king's hands for his extraordinary charges. This would be improper, and very dangerous to the king. For then such

---

[73] This title was first adopted by Gregory the Great, see W. Ullmann, *The Growth of Papal Government in the Middle Ages* (London, 1955), 37.
[74] I Corinthians 9:7.
[75] Matthew 10:10.
[76] Galatians 6:6.
[77] Bodleian Digby MS 145 has 'two of the greatest'.

a lord may spend more than the king, considering that he is charged with no such charges, extraordinary or ordinary, as is the king, except a household, which is but little in comparison of the king's house.[78] Wherefore if this is the case, it shall be necessary, that there be purveyed for the king much greater livelihood than he yet has. For man's courage is so noble, that he naturally aspires to high things and to be exalted, and therefore forces himself to be always greater and greater. For which the Philosopher says, 'of all things we love most to rule'.[79] Whereof it has happened that often, when a subject has had as great a livelihood as his prince, he has before long aspired to the estate of his prince, which may soon be got by such a man. For the rest of the subjects of such a prince, seeing that if so mighty a subject might obtain the estate of their prince, they should then be under a prince twice as mighty as was their old prince – which increase any subject desires, for his own discharge of that which he bears to the sustenance of his prince – will therefore be very glad to help such a subject in his rebellion. And also such an enterprise is the more feasible, when such a rebel has more riches than his sovereign lord. For the people will go with him who may best sustain and reward them. This manner of doing has been so often practised in almost every realm, that their chronicles are full of it.

In the realm of France their king has never been changed, since it was first inhabited by French men, other than by the rebellion of such mighty subjects; such as Childeric[80] king of France, who was descended of Clovis,[81] the first Christian king of France, and who was put down by Pepin son to Charles Martel,[82] who was the most mighty subject that up to that time was ever seen in the realm

---

[78] See Myers, *The Household of Edward IV*.

[79] This is a misreading or alteration of *Auctoritates*, 262, taken from Aristotle, *Politics* VII.xvii.13: 'we always prefer that which we come across first'.

[80] Childeric III was deposed by Pippin the Short in 751 AD, the Carolingian line thereby replacing the Merovingian. He is mentioned in this context in pseudo-Aquinas, *De Regimine Principum*, III.x and in Vincent of Beauvais, *On the Moral Education of a Prince*, ch. 4.

[81] Clovis, king of the Franks, converted to Christianity in 496 AD. He is also mentioned in pseudo-Aquinas, *De Regimine Principum*, II.xvi, see Bloch, *The Royal Touch*, 76–8.

[82] Charles Martel (*c.* 688–741). Frankish Mayor of the palace and illegitimate son of Pepin of Herstal. Martel's son became Pepin III, king of the Franks (751–68).

of France. And afterwards, Charles[83] descended of Charlemagne, son to the said Pepin by nine or by ten generations, was put from the kingdom of France by Hugh Capet,[84] son to Hugh Magnus, earl of Paris, who then was the mightiest subject of France, and was therefore created and called 'Leader of France'. And in our days we have seen a subject of the French kings in such might, that he has given battle to the same king, and put him to flight, and afterwards beseiged him being in Paris his greatest city, and so kept there, until the time this said king had made such end with him, his adherents and followers, as he desired.[85]

We have also seen recently in our realm, some of the king's subjects give him battle, by occasion that their livelihood and offices were the greatest of the land, and otherwise they would not have done so.[86] The earls of Leicester and Gloucester, who were the greatest lords of England, rose against their king Henry III, and took him and his son prisoners in the field.[87] Dreading this manner of conduct to be practised in his land, the last king of the Scots[88] put out of the same land the Earl Douglas whose livelihood and might was almost equivalent to his own, moved thereto by no other cause, save only fear of his rebellion.[89] The chronicles of every realm, and especially of Spain and Denmark, are full of such examples, and so are also the Books of Kings in holy scripture,[90] wherefore it is not necessary to write more here.

And also it may not be eschewed, but that the great lords of the land by reason of new descents falling unto them, and also of marriages, purchases, and other titles, shall often grow to be greater than they are now, and perhaps some of them to be of livelihood

---

[83] Charles the Great or Charlemagne (742–814) was king of the Franks and first Holy Roman Emperor. The last Carolingian king was, in fact, Louis V (966–987) who was succeeded by Hugh Capet. The 'Charles' to whom Fortescue refers may have been Charles of Lotharingia who made a claim to the throne in 988.

[84] Hugh Capet (*c.* 938–996) king of France and founder of the third Frankish royal dynasty, the Capetians.

[85] This is a reference to Charles the Bold, the War of the Public Weal and the treaty of Conflans 1465, see Commynes, *Memoirs*, I.2–14.

[86] The examples closest to those represented here are Clarence and Warwick, but this could also include York and the earl of Salisbury.

[87] Simon de Montfort and Gilbert Clare, the battle of Lewes May 14th, 1264.

[88] James II was killed at the siege of Roxburgh Castle, 1460.

[89] See M. Lynch, *Scotland A New History* (London, 1991), 166–70.

[90] The 'Books of Kings' refers to I and II Samuel and I and II Kings.

and power like a king, which shall be very good for the land so long as they aspire to none higher estate.[91] For such was the duke of Lancaster, who made war upon the king of Spain, one of the mightiest kings of Christendom, in his own realm.[92]

But this is written only to the intent that it is well understood how necessary it is that the king has great possessions and peculiar livelihood for his own safety, above all, when any of his lords shall happen to be so excessively great, as there might thereby grow peril to his estate. For certainly there may no greater peril grow to a prince, than to have a subject of equal power to himself.

Chapter 10
How the crown is best to be endowed

Now that the likeness of the king's ordinary and extraordinary charges are shown, and moreover, how necessary it is that he has great livelihood over and above the same charges, in which it is necessary that he exceed greatly every man of the land, which livelihood undoubtedly he does not presently have, it is therefore useful for us now to inquire how the king may have such livelihood. But first, of what commodities it may best be taken.

The king of France at one time could not spend of his domains in lordships and other patrimony peculiar, as much as could the king of England. This may be clearly seen in the fact that the queen of France has but five thousand marks yearly to her dower, whereas the queen of England has ten thousand marks.[93] For in those days there was little more of the realm of France in the king's hands, than that part which is called the Isle of France. For all the rest of the realm such as Burgundy, Normandy, Guienne, Champagne, Languedoc and Flanders, with many other such great lordships, were in the hands of the Douzepers[94] and of other princes and great lords.

---

[91] This is a reference to the earl of Warwick.

[92] John of Gaunt (1340–99) duke of Lancaster.

[93] Ten thousand marks was the dowry granted to Margaret of Anjou (*Rot. Parl.*, v.118) as it had been to Joanna, wife of Henry IV and Katherine, wife of Henry V.

[94] This is a reference to the 'Twelve Peers' – the archbishop of Rheims, the bishops of Laôn, Langres, Beauvais, Chalons and Noyon, the dukes of Normandy, Burgundy and Aquitaine and the counts of Toulouse, Flanders and Champagne.

For which cause the gabelle of the salt,[95] and the quatrime of the wines[96] were granted to the king by the three estates of France. And this was no little subsidy, for no man in France may eat salt, unless he buys it from the king, and that is now set to so great price, that the bushel, which the king buys for three or four pence, is sold to his people for two shillings and a penny, and sometimes more. And the fourth pipe of the wines which is made in France may be no little thing, since the tilling of the vines is the greatest commodity of the realm, but that commodity we have not in this land.

Wherefore there is no part of the manners of subsidy that might be good for our sovereign lord, unless he might sell to his subjects the salt that comes hither, in which thing he shall have more grumbling of the people than profit. In France the people salt but little meat, except their bacon, for they want to buy little salt, but yet they are compelled to buy more salt than they want. For the king's officers bring to their houses every year, as much salt as by their conjecture is reasonable to the number of men, women and children who live there, for which they shall pay even though they do not want to have so much. This rule would be sore abhorred in England, both by the merchants who are used to having their freedom in buying and selling of salt, and by the people who salt their meats much more than do the Frenchmen, by occasion whereof they will then at every meal grumble at the king who deals with them more rigorously than his progenitors have done. And so his highness shall have thereof, no more than had the man who sheared his hog – much cry and little wool.

In Flanders, and in other lordships from that of the dukes of Burgundy downward, he takes certain impositions made by himself upon every ox, every sheep, and upon other things sold, and also upon every vessel of wine, every barrel of beer, and other victuals sold in his lordships, which is no little revenue to him. But yet he does it in spite of the people, who God defend that the king our sovereign lord should do upon his people, without their grants or

---

[95] The gabelle or salt tax was first imposed by Philip the Fair, 1331, to meet the expenses of the war with England and was formalised in 1342. The compulsory sale of salt was begun by Charles V. See Shennan, *Government and Society*, 52–3, Guenée, *States and Rulers*, 99–101 and Gaussin, *Louis XI* 177–89.
[96] See Gaussin, *Louis XI*, 178.

assent. Nevertheless, with their assent such manner of subsidy, if there could not be found a better way to increase the king's revenues, is not unreasonable. For therein and in the gabelle of the salt, every man shall bear the charge thereof equally. But yet I do not want such a new charge to be put upon the people in our sovereign lord's days, a charge with which his progenitors never charged them, if a better remedy could be found.

King Solomon charged his people with greater impositions than they were accustomed to bear before his days, and because his son King Rehoboam would not ease them thereof, the ten parts of the people, divided into twelve parts, departed from him, and chose themselves a new king, and never again came under his subjection.[97] Of which departing God said himself afterwards, 'this thing is from me',[98] which is an example that it is not good for a king to burden his people excessively.

Wherefore, I believe that if the king might have his livelihood for the sustenance of his estate in great lordships, manors, fee-farms, and such other desmesnes, his people not being charged, he should keep to him wholly their hearts, exceed in lordships all the lords of his realm, and none of them would grow to be like to him, which thing is most to be feared of all the world. For then within few years there should not remain lordships in his realm, by which they might grow so great. Nor might they grow such by marriages, unless if the king willed it.

For to him fall all the great marriages of his land, which he may dispose as he wishes. And it is unlikely that by descent greater heritage shall fall to any man than to the king. For the most and greatest lords of the realm are his cousins. Neither by escheats may so much land fall to any man as to the king, because no man has as many tenants as he, and also no man may have the escheats of treason but himself.[99] And by purchase, if this is done, there shall no man so well increase his livelihood as the king, for none of his tenants shall alienate livelihood without his licence,[100] wherein he may best prefer himself.

---

[97] I Kings 12.
[98] I Kings 12.
[99] See Plucknett, *Concise History*, 536 and Bellamy, *The Law of Treason in England in the Middle Ages*.
[100] See Plucknett, *Concise History*, 539–41 and Simpson, *An Introduction to the History of Land Law* (Oxford, 1961) 48–53.

Nor shall any livelihood be kept as whole as the king's, considering that he may not honestly sell his land, as other men may do, and also his selling would be the hurt of all his realm. Such was the selling of Chirk and Chirk's lands,[101] whereof no precedent has ever been seen, and God defend that any man may see more such hereafter. For selling of a king's livelihood is properly called dilapidation of his crown, and therefore is of great infamy. Now we have found undoubtedly, what manner revenue is best for the endowment of the Crown. But since it is said before, that the king has not at this day sufficient thereto, it is most convenient that we now inquire, how his highness may have sufficient of such revenues, which we have now found best therefore.

Chapter 11
Here is shown, what of the king's livelihood given away, may best be taken again

The holy patriarch Joseph, while he, under Pharaoh, governed the land of Egypt, ruled and so treated the people thereof, that they granted to pay, and paid to the same king, the fifth part of their grains, and of all other things that grew to them yearly of the earth; which charge they bear yet, and ever shall bear.[102] Wherefore their prince, who is now the sultan of Babylon,[103] is one of the mightiest princes of the world; and that notwithstanding the same Egyptians are the richest commons that live under any prince. Whereby we are taught that it shall not only be good for our prince, but also for ourselves, that he is well endowed; for else the patriarch would not have made such a treaty. The French king in one thing, that is to say in wine, takes more of his people than does the sultan; for he takes the fourth penny thereof.[104] But yet he takes nothing of their grains, wools, or any other goods which grow to them of their land.

The king our sovereign lord had in earlier times, since he reigned upon us, livelihood in lordships, lands, tenements, and rents, almost

---

[101] This refers to the castle and lordship of Chirk in Denbighshire which belonged originally to the Mortimers. Henry V bought it in 1418, but in 1438 Henry VI sold it to Cardinal Beaufort.
[102] Genesis 47:26.
[103] The reigning sultan of Babylon was Quayt-Bay (1467–1495).
[104] See Gaussin, *Louis XI*, 178.

to the value of the fifth part of his realm, over and above the possessions of the Church.[105] Of which livelihood, if it had abided still in his hands, he had been more mighty in good revenues than any of the said two kings, or any king who now reigns upon Christian men.

But this was not possible to have been done, for the heirs of those who once owned it are restored to some parts thereof, some by reason of entails,[106] some by reason of other titles, which the king has considered and thought them good and reasonable. And some of the said livelihood his good grace has given to such as have served him notably, that as their renown will be eternal, so it befitted the king's magnificence to make their rewards everlasting in their heirs, to their perpetual memory and honour. And also the king has given part of his livelihood to his most worshipful brothers, who not only have served him in the manner aforesaid, but who are also so close in blood to his highness, that it would not have befitted his magnificence to have done otherwise.[107]

Nevertheless some men have done him service, for which it was reasonable that his grace rewarded them, and for lack of money, the king then rewarded them with land. To some men he has done likewise above their merits, through importunity of their suits. And it is supposed that some of them have received £100 worth of land, who would have held themselves content with £200 in money, if they might have had it in hand.

Wherefore it is thought, that if such gifts, and particularly those which have been made inconsiderately, or above the merits of those who have them, were reformed,[108] and those rewarded with money, or offices, and some with livelihood for term of life, which after their deaths would then return to the Crown, the king should have such livelihood as we now seek for, sufficient for the maintenance

---

[105] See Wolffe, *The Crown Lands*, 15–28.

[106] Entails or estates tail were created by the statute *De Donis Conditionalibus*, the first chapter of the Statute of Westminster (1285), see Plucknett, *Concise History*, 551–2.

[107] If Fortescue is referring to Henry VI, these would be his half-brothers, Edmund Tudor, earl of Richmond, and Jasper Tudor, earl of Pembroke, but he is far more likely to mean Edward IV's brothers George, duke of Clarence and Richard, duke of Gloucester.

[108] Fortescue goes on to state (below, ch.14, 112) that this can only properly be done by means of a general resumption.

of his estate. And if it were not too great, I hold it for undoubted, that the people of this land will be well willing to grant him a subsidy, upon such commodities of his realm as have before been specified, and shall make good that which he lacks of such livelihood; so that his highness will establish the same livelihood then remaining, to abide perpetually to his crown, without translating thereof to any other use. For else when that shall happen hereafter to be given away, his commons will have to be charged with a new subsidy, and thus be kept always in poverty.

Chapter 12
Here is shown what harm would come to England, if the commons thereof were poor

Some men have said that it would be good for the king, if the commons of England were to be made poor, as are the commons of France. For then they would not rebel, as they now often do but which the commons of France do not, nor can do, for they have no weapons, nor armour, nor goods with which to buy it.

To these men it may be said, with the Philosopher, *ad pauca respicientes de facili enunciant*, that is to say, they that see but few things will soon say their advices.[109] Forsooth these folk little consider the good of the realm of England, whereof the might stands most upon the archers, who are not rich men. And if they were to be made poorer than they are, they should not have the wherewithal to buy themselves bows, arrows, padded tunics, or any other armour of defence, whereby they might be able to resist our enemies, when they wish to come upon us. And this they may do on every side, considering that we are an island and, as is said before, we may not readily have succour of any other realm.

Wherefore we shall be a prey to all our enemies, unless we are mighty of ourselves, which might stands most upon our poor archers. Therefore they need not only have such equipment as is now spoken of, but also they need to be much exercised in shooting, which may not be done without very great expenses, as every man expert therein knows very well. Wherefore the making poor of the

---

[109] *Auctoritates Aristotelis*, 167, from Aristotle, *On Generation and Corruption*, I.2.10.

commons, which is the making poor of our archers, shall be the destruction of the greatest might of our realm.[110]

Likewise, if poor men may not easily rise up, as is the opinion of these men who for that reason would have the commons poor; how then, if a mighty man made a rising should he be repressed, when all the commons are so poor, that after such opinion they may not fight, and by that reason not help the king with fighting? And why does the king have the commons mustered every year if it is good that they have no harness nor are able to fight?[111] O, how unwise is the opinion of these men, for it may not be maintained by any reason!

Likewise, before now, when any rising has been made in this land by the commons, the poorest men have been the greatest causers and doers therein. And prosperous men have been loth thereto, for fear of losing their goods. But yet often they have gone with them, because of the threat that otherwise the same poor men would have taken their goods. Wherein it seems that poverty has been the whole cause of all such risings. The poor man has been stirred thereto by occasion of his poverty, in order to get goods, and the rich men have gone with them, because they did not want to be made poor by losing their goods. What then would happen, if all the commons were poor? Truly it is likely that this land then should be like the realm of Bohemia, where the commons, because of poverty, rose upon the nobles, and made all their goods to be common.[112]

Likewise, it is the king's honour, and also his duty, to make his realm rich; and it is dishonour when he has but a poor realm, of which men will say that he reigns only upon beggars.[113] Yet it would be much greater dishonour, if he found his realm rich, and then made it poor. And it would also be greatly against the conscience of he who ought to defend them and their goods, if he took from

---

[110] 12 Richard II ch.6 stated that all servants and labourers should have bows and arrows and should practise shooting on Sundays. This statute was re-enforced by 11 Henry IV, ch.4. Cf. Ashby, *Active Policy of a Prince*: 'By law every man should be compeled / To use the bow and shooting for disport', 11.569–70 and Lydgate and Burgh's *Secrees*: 'look you be kept well with good archers', 1.2431.

[111] Under the Statute of Winchester the constables of every hundred were obliged to inspect armour twice a year.

[112] This is a reference to the Hussite wars 1419–1436.

[113] Cf. Giles of Rome, *On Princely Government*, III.ii.8.

them their goods without lawful cause. From the infamy whereof God defend our king, and give him grace to augment his realm in riches, wealth, and prosperity, to his perpetual laudation and worship.

Likewise, the realm of France never gives any subsidy to their [*sic*] prince freely of their own good will, because the commons thereof are so poor, that they may not give anything of their own goods. And the king there never asks for subsidy from his nobles, for fear that if he thus charged them, they would enter into an alliance with the commons, and perhaps put him down. But our commons are rich, and therefore they give to their king, sometimes fifteenths and tenths,[114] and often other great subsidies, when he needs them for the good and defence of his realm. How great a subsidy was it, when the realm gave to their king a fifteenth and a tenth for five years,[115] and the ninth fleece of their wools, and also the ninth sheaf of their grains, for the term of five years. This they would not have been able to do, if they had been impoverished by their king, as are the commons of France. Such a grant has never been made by any realm of Christendom, of which any chronicle makes mention, nor is any other able to or has cause to do so. For they do not have as much freedom in their own goods,[116] nor are they treated by such favourable laws as we are, except in a few regions before specified.

Likewise, we see daily, how men who have lost their goods, and have fallen into poverty, soon become robbers and thieves; which would not have been the case, if poverty had not brought them thereto. How many thieves are there likely to be in this land, if all the commons were poor? The greatest safety, truly, and also the most honour that may come to the king is that his realm should be rich in every estate. For nothing shall make his people arise, except lack of goods or lack of justice. But yet certainly when they lack goods they will arise, saying that they lack justice. Nevertheless if they are not poor, they will never arise, unless their prince so leaves justice, that he gives himself all to tyranny.

---

[114] See J.A.F. Thomson, *The Transformation of Medieval England 1370–1529*, 259–62.

[115] There are no extant records of such a grant.

[116] Cf. Aquinas, *On Princely Government*, I.X.

Chapter 13
Only lack of heart and cowardice keep the Frenchmen from rising

Poverty is not the reason why the commons of France do not rise against their sovereign lord. For there were never poorer people in that land, than were the commons of the country of Caux in our time, which was then almost barren for lack of farmers; as it now well appears by the new husbandry that is done there, namely in digging and uprooting of trees, bushes, and groves, grown while we were lords of the country. And yet the said commons of Caux made a marvellous great rising, and took our towns, castles, and fortresses, and slew our captains and soldiers, at such a time as we had but few men of war lying in that country.[117] Which proves that it is not poverty which keeps Frenchmen from rising, but it is cowardice and lack of hearts and courage, which no Frenchman has like an English man.[118]

It has often been seen in England, that three or four thieves have, because of poverty, set upon six or seven honest men, and robbed them all. But it has not been seen in France, that six or seven thieves have been tough enough to rob three or four honest men. Wherefore it is very seldom that Frenchmen are hanged for robbery, for they have no hearts to do so terrible an act. There are therefore more men hanged in England in a year for robbery and manslaughter, than are hanged in France for such crimes in seven years. There is no man hanged for robbery in Scotland for seven years at a stretch. And yet they are often hanged for larceny, and stealing of goods in the absence of the owner thereof.[119] And their hearts serve them not to take a man's goods while he is present and will defend them; which manner of taking is called robbery.

But the English man is of another courage. For if he is poor, and sees another man having riches which may be taken from him by force, he will not spare to do so, unless that poor man is very honest. Wherefore it is not poverty, but it is lack of heart and cowardice which keeps the Frenchmen from rising.

[117] The Caux rising took place in 1435.
[118] This statement is perhaps a legacy of Agincourt.
[119] See Bellamy, *Criminal Law and Society*.

Chapter 14
Here it is shown, why it is necessary for there to be a resumption and a grant of goods made to the king

This inquiry which we now have made, in order to understand how harmful it would be to the king, and to his realm, if his commons were poor, has been a digression from the matter in which we labour, that is to say, to seek to understand how the king may best have sufficient and everlasting livelihood for the maintenance of his estate. Wherefore it is necessary that we now return to the point at which we left, which, as I remember, was this.

We found by many great reasons, that it was necessary that all such gifts as have been made from the king's livelihood without due consideration, being not deserved or above the merits of those who have received them, should be reformed, so that those who have done any service, should not be unrewarded. Which thing, I believe, may not be perfectly done, without a general resumption, made by authority of parliament and also that there should be given to the king by the same authority, a great subsidy,[120] with which his highness, by the advice of his council,[121] may reward those who have deserved rewards, but who ought not therefore to have part of the revenues by which his estate must needs be maintained, or at least ought not to have as much of the revenues as they have now, or not as great an estate in the same.[122]

Considering that all such giving away of the king's livelihood is harmful to all his liegemen, who shall thereby, as is before shown, be compelled to a new charge for the maintenance of his estate. But yet, before any such resumption is made, it would be good if a worshipful and a notable council should be established, by the advice of which all new gifts and rewards may be moderated and made, as if no such gifts or rewards had been made before this time. Provided always, that no man is harmed, by reason of such resumption, in the arrears of such livelihood as he shall then have,

---

[120] For the numerous acts of resumption and their exemptions, see Wolffe, *Crown Lands* and his 'Acts of Resumption in Lancastrian Parliaments', *EHR* 73 (1958).
[121] On the council, see Appendix B and below, chs. 15 and 16.
[122] Different types of 'estates' could be given in lands, for example in fee-simple or for a term of years.

which shall run after that resumption, and before the said new gifts and rewards.

And when such a council is fully created and established, it shall be good that all supplications which shall be made to the king for any gift or reward, are sent to the same council, and there debated and deliberated, firstly as to whether the supplicant has deserved such a reward as he asks, and, if he has deserved it, it is yet necessary to deliberate as to whether the king may give such a reward as he asks from his revenues, saving to himself sufficient for the maintenance of his estate. For otherwise such giving would be no virtue, but a kind of prodigality,[123] and as such, it would be delapidation of his crown.

Wherefore no private person will, by reason of liberality or of reward, so abate his own livelihood, that he may not keep such an estate as he did before. And truly it were better, that a private person should lack his reward which he has well deserved, than that by his reward the public good and all the land were hurt.[124]

Wherefore to eschew these two harms, the council may then advise how such a person may be rewarded with office, money, marriage, franchises, privilege, or such other things, of which the Crown has great riches. And truly if this order is kept, the king shall not be grieved by importunity of suitors, nor shall they, by importunity or brokerage, obtain any unreasonable desires.[125] O what quiet shall grow to the king by this order; and in what rest shall then his people live, having no cause for complaint with such as shall be about his person, as they used to have, for the giving away of his land, and also for the miscounselling of him in many other cases; nor of murmur against the king's person, for the misgovernance of his realm!

For in this council every difficult case may be determined, before the king does anything therein. And the wise man says, 'where there

---

[123] One of the standard pieces of advice in the mirror-for-princes literature was the need to hit the mean between avarice and prodigality, see Genet, *Four English Political Tracts* for examples.

[124] Here is clearly stated the priority of the public good of the realm over the private interest of any of its members, including the 'rex regnans'.

[125] Cf. 'Take you to live of your own property / Of your revenues, livelihood and rent / Proportioning after the quantity / Your expenses by your own judgement / Paying all that is to your estate lent / Thus you shall our lord God and the world please / And all men are pleased to leave you at your ease', Ashby, *Active Policy of a Prince*, stanza 40.

are many counsels, there is well-being';[126] and truly such a continual council may well be called, 'many counsels', for it is frequent, and counsels every day.

Chapter 15
How the king's council may be chosen and established

The king's council used to be chosen from great princes, and from the greatest lords of the land, both spiritual and temporal, and also other men that were in great authority and offices, which lords and officers had almost as many matters of their own to be treated in the council, as had the king. Wherefore, when they came together, they were so occupied with their own matters, and with the matters of their kin, servants, and tenants, that they intended but little, and at other times not at all, to the king's matters.[127]

And also there were few matters of the king which did not also touch the said counsellors, their cousins, their servants, tenants, or such other as they owed favour to. And what lower man was there sitting in that council, who dared speak against the opinion of any of the great lords? And why, then, might not some men corrupt some of the servants and counsellors of some of the lords in order to move the lords to partiality, and to make them as favourable and partial as were the same servants, or the parties who moved them in that way?

Then no matter treated in the council could be kept secret. For the lords often told their own counsellors and servants, who made suit to them for those matters, how they had fared in them, and who was against them. How may the king be counselled by such great lords to restrain the giving away of his land and the giving of offices, corrodies, or pensions of abbeys,[128] to other men's servants, since they most desire such gifts for themselves, and their servants?

Which things considered, and also many others which shall be shown hereafter, it is thought good, that the king should have a

---

[126] Proverbs 11:14.
[127] See Baldwin, *The King's Council*.
[128] See below, n.144.

council chosen and established in the following form, or in some other like form.

First, that there should be chosen twelve spiritual men, and twelve temporal men, from the wisest and best disposed men that can be found in all the parts of this land; and that they shall be sworn to counsel the king after a form to be devised for their oath. And in particular, that they shall take no fee, nor clothing, nor rewards from any man, except only from the king; just as the justices of the King's Bench, and of the Common Pleas are sworn, when they take their offices.[129] And that these twenty-four shall always be councillors, unless any fault is found in them, or unless the king wishes, by the advice of the majority of them, to change any of them. And that every year there shall be chosen by the king four lords spiritual, and four lords temporal, to be for that year of the same council, in like form as the said twenty-four shall be. And that they shall all have a head, or a chief to rule the council, one of the said twenty-four, and chosen by the king, having his office at the king's pleasure, who may then be called, *Capitalis consiliarius*.

It shall not be necessary, for the twelve spiritual men of this council, to have as great wages as the twelve temporal men, because they shall not need to keep a household in their country, while they are absent, as the temporal men must needs do for their wives and children. By which consideration the spiritual judges in the court of parlement of Paris, take only two hundred francs a year, whereas the temporal judges thereof take 300 francs a year.[130]

Also, the said eight lords who, by reason of their baronies and estates, are 'natural-born counsellors' to the king and therefore ought to counsel him at all times whenever he wills it, need not have great wages for their attendance at his council, which shall last but for a year. For temporal men who, by reason of their inheritance and livelihood, are made sheriffs for a year,[131] take from the king little, and almost nothing, for their service of that year.

And though the wages of the said twenty-four councillors seem to be a new and a great charge to the king, yet when it is considered, what great wages the great lords and other men, who were of the

---

[129] The form of the oath was prescribed by *Rot. Parl.* 20 Edward II, the oath is printed in Chrimes, *De laudibus*, 204.

[130] Cf. 'Articles', Appendix C, 3.

[131] On sheriffs, see note 118 to *In Praise of the Laws of England*, ch. XXIV, 35.

king's council in times past, took for their attendance thereto, which manner of council was nothing so useful to the king and to his realm as this will be, which wages shall thenceforth cease, the wages of the twenty-four councillors shall appear no great charge to the king. And I can suppose, that some kings before this time, have given to some one man who has served him, as much livelihood yearly, as the said wages will come to. And if the same wages are thought to be too great a charge to the king, the aforesaid councillors can be fewer in number, so as to be sixteen councillors of private persons, with two lords spiritual, and two lords temporal, so that they are then only twenty persons in all.

These councillors are able continually, at such hours as shall be assigned to them, to consult and deliberate upon matters of difficulty which appertain to the king; and then upon the matters of the policy of the realm;[132] as how the export of the money may be restrained, how bullion may be brought in to the land, how also plate, jewels, and money recently borne out, may be recovered; of which very wise men can soon find the means.[133] And also how the prices of merchandise grown in this land may be sustained and increased, and the prices of merchandise brought in to this land abated.[134] Also, how our navy may be maintained and augmented, and upon such other points of policy, to the greatest profit and increase, that ever came to this land. How also the laws may be amended in such things as they need reformation in, wherefore the parliaments shall be able to do more good in a month to the mending of the law, than they shall be able to do in a year, if the amending thereof be not debated, and by such council ripened to their hands.

There may be of this council, when they wish to come thereto, or when they are desired by the said councillors, the great officers of the land, such as chancellor, treasurer, and privy seal, of which the chancellor, when he is present, may be president, and have the supreme rule of all the council. Also the judges, the barons of the exchequer, the clerk of the rolls, and such lords as the aforesaid councillors will desire to be with them for matters of great difficulty,

---

[132] Cf. 'The Libelle of English Polycye' which is discussed in Jacob, *The Fifteenth Century*, 346–9.

[133] See Thomson, *Transformation of Medieval England*, ch.7.

[134] See Thomson, *Transformation of Medieval England*, ch.7 and Tables A:2 and A:3.

may be of this council when they be so desired, and otherwise not.

All other matters which shall concern this council, such as when a councillor dies how a new councillor shall be chosen, how many hours of the day this council shall sit, when they shall have any vacation, how long any of them may be absent, and how he shall have his leave, with all other articles necessary for the ordering and rule of this council, can be conceived at leisure, and put in a book, and that book kept in this council as a register or an ordinary of how they shall act in all things.[135]

Chapter 16
How the Romans prospered whilst they had a great council[136]

The Romans, whilst their council, called the senate, was great, got, through the wisdom of that council, the lordship of a great part of the world.[137] And afterwards Julius, their first emperor, counselled by the same senate, got the monarchy of almost the whole world. Wherefore Octavian, their second emperor, commanded all the world to be described as subject unto him.[138] But after this, when ill-disposed emperors, such as Nero, Domitian, and others had slain a great part of the senators, and scorned the council of the senate, the estate of the Romans and of their emperors began to fall down, and has fallen away since, into such decay, that now the lordships of the emperor are not as great, as are the lordships of some one king, who, while the senate was whole, was subject to the emperor.

By which example it is thought, that if the king should have such a council as is before specified, his land shall not only be rich and wealthy, as were the Romans, but also his highness shall be mighty, and of power to subdue his enemies, and all others upon whom he shall wish to reign. Many of the books of chronicles are full of such

---

[135] Cf. *Rot. Parl.* v.283.

[136] This chapter is to be compared with Appendix B, below.

[137] On the Roman Senate, see Jolowicz, *Historical Introduction to the Study of Roman Law* (2nd edn, Cambridge, 1952) 27–43. Fortescue may have derived his conception of this body from I Maccabees 8:1–7 or pseudo-Aquinas, *De Regimine Principum*, IV.i or xxv.

[138] Luke 2:1.

examples, and especially the chronicles of the Lacedemonians, and of the Athenians, who, while they prospered, were best counselled, and did the most by means of council, of any people of the world, except the Romans. But when they left such council, they fell into non-power and poverty; as of the city of Athens it may well appear from the fact that it is now but a poor village, and once was the most worshipful city of Greece.

Chapter 17
Here follow instructions for the giving of the king's offices

If it will please the king to give no office, until the time that his intent therein is shared with his council, and their opinion by his highness understood in the same, he shall be able so to reward his servants with offices, as there shall be little need to give them much of his livelihood, and his offices shall then be given to such as shall only serve himself [the king]. Wherefore he shall have then a greater might, and protection of his officers, when he wishes to call them, than he now has of his other feedmen under the estate of lords.

For the might of the land, next after the might of the great lords thereof, stands most in the king's officers. For they can best rule the countries where their offices are, which is in every part of the land. A poor bailiff may do more in his bailiwick, than any man of his degree dwelling within his office. Some forester of the king's, who has no other livelihood, may bring more men to the field well arrayed, especially for shooting, than may some knight or squire of very great livelihood, dwelling by him, and having no office. What then may greater officers do – stewards of great lordships, receivers, constables of castles, master foresters, and such other officers, besides the higher officers, as justices of forests, justices and chamberlains of countries, the warden of the ports, and such other?[139]

Forsooth it is not easily estimable, what might the king may have of his officers, if each of them had but one office, and served no other man but the king. Nor is it easy to estimate, how many men

---

[139] Details of many of these officers can be found in the *Black Book* of Edward IV, see Myers, *The Household of Edward IV.*

may be rewarded with offices, and how greatly, if they are given with discretion.

The king gives more than a thousand offices, besides those that my lord the prince gives, whose officers I reckon to be the king's officers. Of these officers some may spend yearly, by reason of his office, £200, some £100, some 100 marks, some £40, some 50 marks, and so on downwards. So that the least of them, although he be only a parker, taking but two pence a day, yet he has yearly £3 and 10 pence, besides his dwelling in the lodge, his cow for his milk, and such other things going about him, and the fees of his office, so that that office is to him as profitable as would be 100 shillings of fee or rent, which is a fair living for a yeoman.[140]

How many men then of every estate, and of every degree, and how greatly, may the king reward with offices, without giving away of his livelihood? Forsooth the livelihood of the greatest lord in England may not suffice to reward so many men, though he would divide every bit of it amongst his servants, nor may the two greatest lords of England make as great a might as the king may have solely of his officers, if they were wholly and only his servants, and each of them had but one office.

To this say such lords and other men who ask of the king offices for their servants, that they and all their servants shall always serve the king, and his officers shall do him the better service, because they are in their service; for they will help him to do so, and suffer none in their company but such as will do so. To which it may be said, that it is true that they shall do the king service while they are in their company; but they would have done so even if the king had never made them his officers. Wherefore the king shall not be the better served, because he has given his offices to their servants, but rather the worse. For our Lord said, 'No-one can serve two lords'.[141] And so the king shall lose the offices, as for any particular service he shall have for them, or that the same officers should think themselves beholden to the king for their offices, which his highness has given them in consideration of their masters, and for no reward of any service that they have done, or shall do to himself.

By consideration whereof their old masters shall be better served by them than they were before, and so be more mighty in their

---

[140] See C. Dyer, *Standards of Living in the Later Middle Ages*.
[141] Matthew 6:24.

countries to do what they wish; and the king shall be in less might, and have the fewer officers to repress them when they do amiss. And this has caused many men to be such brokers and suitors to the king, in order to have his offices in their countries for themselves, and for their men, that almost no man in some country dares take an office of the king, unless he first has the good will of the said brokers and engrossers of offices,[142] for if he did not so, he should not after that time have peace in his country. Whereof has come and grown many great troubles and debates in divers countries of England.

Which matters thoroughly considered, it truly seems good, that no man should have any office of the king's gift, unless he is first sworn that he is servant to no other man, nor will serve any other man, nor take his clothing or fee while he serves the king. And that no man should have more offices than one, except the king's brothers who can have two offices, and such men as serve the king about his person, or in his council, who can have in their countries a parkership for their disport when they come home, or another such office, as they may keep well by their deputies.[143]

Chapter 18
Instruction how corrodies and pensions may best be given

And if it will please the king to give no corrody nor pension,[144] which he has by right of his crown of every abbey, priory, and other houses founded upon hospitality by any of his progenitors, until the time that his intent therein be shared and deliberated with his aforesaid council, and that his highness shall have understood their opinion in the same; then shall men of his household be rewarded with corrodies, and have honest sustenance in their old age when they may no longer serve; and the clerks of his chapel[145] who have wives, or who are not advanced, shall be rewarded with

---

[142] See Wolffe, *The Crown Lands*, 40.
[143] See Introduction, xxxvii.
[144] These were contributions of food or provisions or, more frequently, of money, paid annually by religious houses. For examples, see *Rot. Parl.* v.473.
[145] See Myers, *The Household of Edward IV*

pensions without great abating of the king's revenues, for their rewards or sustenance. For such corrodies and pensions were first given to the king for the same intent. But now recently, other men than the king's servants have asked for them, and by importunate suit have got a great part of them. And this is to the king's great harm and hurt of his said servants, who because of that live in the greater penury, and in no security of their sustenance in the future, when they shall not be able to do the king service.

Chapter 19
How great good will grow of the firm endowing of the Crown

And when the king, by the means aforesaid or otherwise, has recovered his livelihood,[146] if then it would please his most noble grace to establish, and, so to say, amortise the same livelihood to his crown,[147] such that it may never be alienated therefrom, without the assent of his parliament, which then would be as a new foundation of his crown, he shall thereby be the greatest founder of the world. For whereas other kings have founded bishoprics, abbeys, and other houses of religion, the king shall then have founded a whole realm, and endowed it with greater possessions, and better, than ever was any realm in Christendom.

This manner of foundation cannot be against the king's prerogative, or his liberty, any more than is the foundation of an abbey, from which he may take no part of the possessions which he has once given it, without the assent of its convent. But this manner of endowment of his crown shall be to the king a greater prerogative, in that he has then enriched his crown with such riches and possessions, as no king shall ever be able to take from it without the assent of his whole realm.[148]

---

[146] That is, by a general resumption made by an Act of Parliament.

[147] To amortise is to alienate in mortmain, that is, to convey lands or property to an ecclesiastical or any other corporation and its successors. Thus, Fortescue treats the Crown as a corporation. Moreover, he envisages 'a new foundation of the Crown', by which is meant the re-establishment of the institution with an endowment or provision for its perpetual maintenance.

[148] Cf.: 'the common prosperity should not be for any limited period, but should endure, if possible, in perpetuity', Aquinas, *On Princely Government* I.xv.

Nor can this be to the hurt of the prerogative or power of his successors; for, as is shown before, it is no prerogative or power to be able to lose any good, or to be able to waste, or put it away. For all such things come of impotency, as does power to be sick or grow old. And truly, if the king does thus, he shall do thereby daily more alms than shall be done by all the foundations that were ever made in England. For every man of the land shall by this foundation every day be the merrier, the surer and fare the better in his body and all his goods, as every wise man may well conceive.

The foundation of abbeys, of hospitals, and other such houses is nothing in comparison hereof. For this shall be a college,[149] in which shall sing and pray for evermore all the men of England, spiritual and temporal. And their song shall be, among other anthems, such: 'blessed be our Lord God, because he has sent king Edward the fourth to reign upon us.[150] He has done more for us, than any king of England ever did, or might have done before him. The harms which have befallen in the getting of his realm, are now by him turned to our entire good and profit. We shall now be able to enjoy our own goods and live under justice, which we have not done for a long time, God knows.[151] Wherefore of his alms it is that we have all that is in our possession'.

Chapter 20
Instruction for making of patents of gifts

These premises mean only that the king without the assent of his parliament shall give land for term of their lives to such as do him particular service, for thereby his crown may not be dispossessed because that land will soon come again. But then it would be good if the same land is given no more; for otherwise importunate suitors will be greedy for such reversions, and often ask for them before they occur. And when they have occurred, the king shall have no rest with such suitors, until his highness shall have given again all

---

[149] A college is a voluntary, self-governing society with a perpetual endowment, see my Introduction, xxxv. On the founding of colleges, see Jacob, *Fifteenth Century*, 669.

[150] See Introduction, xxxiii.

[151] There is here a strong sense of the need to make proper amends for the war and injustices of the previous reign.

such land as he has once given. By continuance thereof, that land shall not serve him but for gifts, as do offices, corrodies, and pensions.

And truly it would be good if of all the king's gifts his patents[152] made mention that they were passed 'by the advice of his council', especially for a year or two. For if such an order is kept, men will not be so hasty to ask rewards, unless they are of very good merits; and many men will then be of better governance, in order that the king's council should deem them worthy to be rewarded. And those who do not obtain what they desire shall have then little cause for complaint, considering that they lack it by discretion of the king's council. And the king shall have hereby great rest, and be well defended against such importunate suitors. And yet he may leave this order when he wishes to.[153]

---

[152] Gifts of the right to something, given by letters patent.
[153] For a discussion of this last line, see Introduction, xxxviii.

Appendices

Appendix A
Extracts from On the Nature of the Law of Nature

These extracts are from chapters I.xvi, I.xviii and I.xxvi of *De Natura Legis Naturae*. They are slightly amended versions of the translation by Lord Clermont, published in his 1869 edition, volume I

Answer to the second cause of the war above mentioned. But the author first distinguishes the law *(ius)*[1] of a king reigning royally from the law *(ius)* of a king ruling politically and royally[2]

O Samuel, Prophet of the Lord, the Lord did not command you to proclaim to the people of Israel the law of what king soever they pleased, but He Himself, incited to that severity by the inconsiderate request of the people, said to you, 'Hear you their voice, but take them to witness, and tell them beforehand the law of the king *(ius regis)*, not of every king, but of the king who is to reign over

---

[1] There are difficulties in the translation of *ius* in Fortescue's works, but it is perhaps best defined as that which the *dominus* or lord has and imposes on those over whom he is lord. It refers to the power of command and is therefore also connected with *imperium*. Indeed Fortescue often also uses the verb *imperare*. Cf. *Governance* n.10. I have translated it as 'law' because this is the word Fortescue uses in *Governance*, chs.1 and 2.

[2] *On the Nature of the Law of Nature*, I.xvi. The latin is printed in Chrimes, *De laudibus*, 152–3, as well as in Clermont edn, 1869.

them.'[3] Nor did you, the Prophet, set before them the law of a king in general, but following faithfully the command of God, you said to the people, 'This is the law of the king (*ius regis*) who is to rule over you. He shall take your sons and put them in his chariots,' etc.[4]

St Thomas, in the book above mentioned which he wrote to the king of Cyprus, mentioning the various kinds of government which the Philosopher teaches, commends especially for his own part royal dominion and political dominion,[5] which kinds of government Giles of Rome describing in his *On Princely Government*, writes, 'that he is the head of a royal dominion, who is so according to the laws (*leges*) which he himself lays down and according to his own will and pleasure, but he is the head of a political dominion who rules the citizens according to laws which they have established'.[6] But that there is a third kind of dominion, not inferior to these in dignity and honour, which is called the political and royal, we are not only taught by experience and ancient history, but we know has been taught in the doctrine of St Thomas.[7]

For in the kingdom of England the kings make not laws, nor impose subsidies on their subjects, without the consent of the Three Estates of the realm; and even the judges of that realm are all bound by their oaths not to render judgement against the laws of the land (*leges terre*), even if they should have the commands of the prince to the contrary.[8] May not, then, this dominion be called political, that is to say, regulated by the administration of many,[9] and may

---

[3] I Samuel 8:9

[4] I Samuel 8:11.

[5] Thomas Aquinas, *On Princely Government*.

[6] Giles of Rome, *On Princely Government*, III. ii.

[7] It is this particular combination of *dominium politicum et regale* which has not been found in the works of Aquinas nor of Giles of Rome, see my Introduction, above xxiv–xxv. For detailed discussion, see F. Gilbert, 'Fortescue's "dominium regale et politicum"' 88–97 and J.H. Burns, 'Fortescue and the Political Theory of *dominium*' 777–97.

[8] Fortescue himself went against the king in refusing to release one Thomas Kerver in 1447, see Chrimes, *De laudibus*, LXII.

[9] The Latin here is 'plurium dispensatione regulatum'. Clearly some form of participation in government by 'the many' is here envisaged but the precise meaning of 'dispensatione' is less clear. Burns ('Political Theory of *dominium*', 780–3) sees an erosion of the participatory element in government as a result of the examples of Rome and Israel. However, the analogies are intended to be loose and to provide

it not also deserve to be named royal dominion, seeing that the subjects themselves cannot make laws without the authority of the king, and the kingdom, being subject to the king's dignity, is possessed by kings and their heirs successively by hereditary right, in such manner as no dominions are possessed which are only politically regulated.

And in Roman history we are taught that the people first tried royal government under the seven kings, then, because they could no longer endure the indolence, luxury and spoliation of their kings, that, shaking off the royal yoke, they proscribed Tarquin their seventh king and the royal government as well, and, afterwards submitting themselves to a political government, they were ruled for more than five hundred years under consuls and dictators, regulated by decrees of the senate. But at last Julius, being one of the two consuls, impatient of shared dominion, seized for himself alone the monarchy both of the city and of the world, whence from that time he thought to live royally, yet would not be distinguished by the name of king, which was hateful to the Romans, but chose rather to be called emperor, a title which certain of the consuls before affected, when dictators. But he being at last put to death on account of this arrogance, Octavian, a man of the mildest character,[10] being raised to[11] the monarchy of the whole world, governed it not only royally but also politically by the advice of the senate; in like manner did some of the succeeding emperors whose dominion St Thomas in his book above mentioned calls royal and political[12] – royal because what pleased them was law for all their

examples of some form of combination of royal and political government. In England, the combination is that of an hereditary king with Parliament and the ministers of the law (cf. *Praise*, ch.XXXVI, above, 52.) and in *The Governance*, participation is extended to a more representative council, see above, 115 and J. Guy, 'The King's Council and Political Participation' in A. Fox and J. Guy (eds), *Reassessing the Henrician Age*, 121–47.

[10] The word is 'mansuetissimus'. Fortescue uses 'mansuete' as the adjective to describe those who first set up true monarchies, see *Governance*, ch. 2, above 86.

[11] The Latin is 'erectus', as in *Praise*, ch. XIII, above, 20.

[12] It is thought that this may be a reference to pseudo-Aquinas, *De Regimine Principum*, III.12 in which the continuator (Ptolemy of Lucca) defines 'dominium imperiale' as that which is between royal dominion and political dominion ('medium tenet inter politicum et regale') and is therefore in a different, third, category. The idea is more fully worked, out in III.20, see F. Gilbert, 'Fortescue's "dominium regale et politicum" ', 90–2.

subjects,[13] but political, not because they always consulted the senators, for many of the emperors, to their own destruction, despised their advice,[14] but because they ruled the commonwealth (*rempublicam*) for the advantage of the many,[15] namely the Romans, and because the Roman empire did not descend to their own heirs as kingdoms are wont to do.

Thus also the children of Israel, as that Saint says,[16] before they asked for a king, were ruled politically, whence their dominion was political and royal; political, because the Judges under whom they were ruled administered everything for their common advantage, and nothing for the individual advantages of them the judges (whence Samuel, the last of the Judges, offered himself before Saul, the first king of the nation, to answer for everything that he had done in the office of Judge;[17] and how great was then the assembly of the council of that people the Book of Numbers, chapter 16, reveals, seeing that it is written that two hundred and fifty, who were called by their names, were in the council at the sedition of Corah, in which it is evident that none were engaged but those of two tribes, Levi, namely, and Reuben, by which it may be conjectured that there was a great multitude in that council of all the tribes of Israel[18]) and the kingdom of that people was royal, because the King of all kings had ruled it as His own kingdom.[19] In this kingdom, before they had desired a king, it was not lawful for any man to do to another what reason would not suffer him to wish done to himself, nor could one take away the servant or handmaid of another, against his will, nor give another man's field to his servants, as the Prophet says it was the king's right (*ius*) to do. Thus the law which the Prophet proclaimed was not then the law (*lex*)

---

[13] This refers to the 'lex regia' of the Roman law, *CIC Institutes* 1.2.6 and *CIC Digest* 1.4.1. Also used by Fortescue in *Praise*, chs IX and XXXIV, 17 and 48.

[14] Cf. Appendix B and *Governance*, ch. 16 above, 117.

[15] The Latin reads 'ad plurium usum'. This is the point at which Burns sees the erosion of the political element as being most complete, ('Political Theory of *dominium*', 781). However, the crucial element is that it is still government for the common good and not for the good of the rulers.

[16] Pseudo-Aquinas, *De Regimine Principum* II.viii and IX.; cf. *Governance* ch. 1.

[17] Samuel 12:1–5.

[18] Numbers 16:16–19. Note that the number of the council is close to the 250–300 elected representatives in parliament and to the 300 Roman senators, see *Praise*, ch. XVIII., above, 27.

[19] Deuteronomy 14:2, cf. *Governance*, ch. 1, above, 84.

in that kingdom, even as such is not the law (*ius*) in any kingdom politically regulated. Wherefore the Prophet did not say simply and precisely that the law (*lex*) which he promulgated was the law (*ius*) of the king, but he said relatively that it was the law (*ius*) of the king who was to rule over the children of Israel, as if he had said: 'This obstinate and ungrateful people which does not know its own good, shall not henceforth be ruled under a political dominion, nor under a royal and political one, as before, but shall be governed by an only royal dominion, by which, as by a halter and bridle, its obstinacy shall be held in check.'

The law of nature fashioned the estate of the king (*statum regium*) in its beginning, albeit it was the wicked who first established that estate[20]

Think over again, I pray you, Law of the King (*Ius Regis*), and consider in your mind how you heard above most truly declared, that the power of the king took its beginning under and from the law of nature, and by it always was and is regulated; to which it is no objection that wicked men began that power, for although the Jews handed Christ over to His death, God the Father also delivered Him to death by means of them; but the Jews did it for spite, the Father for mercy. In like manner, although the unjust began the kingly highness (*culmen regium*) for ambition, the law of nature began it for the good of mankind by means of those unjust men – they by sin, the law by a most righteous working, so that in one and the same act not only the virtue of justice but the maliciousness of sin contended in the working of the law of nature. Thus also the iniquity of Cain, first for avarice, marked off boundaries on the earth, and the pride of Nimrod first usurped dominion over men, and yet nothing better or more fitting than these things could have befallen the human race, in as much as if all things had remained in common as before, and there had been no dominion over men upon the earth after the fall of man, the commonwealth of mankind (*res publica homini*) would have been less fittingly managed, and for want of justice the human race would have torn itself to pieces in

---

[20] *On the Nature of the Law of Nature* I.xviii. The Latin is printed at Chrimes, *De laudibus*, 156–7 as well as in Clermont edn (1869).

mutual slaughter. For 'the Gentiles', as the Apostle says in Romans, chapter 2, 'although they do not have the law (*legem*), they do by nature the things which are of the law, and not having such a law are a law unto themselves, and they show the workings of the law written in their hearts'.[21]

But as to the manner in which the nations began the power of the king by means of the law of nature, or rather in which the law itself began it by means of the nations,[22] St Thomas in the first book of his treatise *On Princely Government*, is believed to have truly taught when he said, among all things which are co-ordinated into one, something is ever found which is naturally regulative of the other. As, for example, in the corporeal universe, the earthly bodies are regulated by the first body, which is celestial, and the same are governed by the rational creature, and man's body by his soul, and the parts of the soul, that is passion and desire, by reason, and all the members of man's body by the head and the heart.[23] And as it is by nature that man is a social and political animal, living in a multitude (as in the same book is clearly proved)[24], and as everyone naturally makes provision and strives for[25] his private and particular interest, the multitude of human society, if it were not ruled by someone who would bear the charge of it, would waste away and perish, more especially since man's nature has been spoilt by sin, by which it has been made prone to offend.

Hence also, since art, as the Philosopher says, imitates nature so far as it can,[26] nations have constituted rulers for the multitude of their societies, just as nature in everything made up from the union of divers things, constitutes something to rule, and the power of these rulers, because they rule (*regunt*) others, the nations have

---

[21] Romans 2:14–15.

[22] Note the Thomist definition of natural law as both the participation of the eternal law in rational creatures and the participation of rational creatures in the eternal law, see Aquinas, *Summa Theologica* Ia IIae qu.91 art.2 (concl.).

[23] Aquinas, *On Princely Government* I.i. Aquinas states that some say the body is ruled by the head, others by the heart but Fortescue says here that it is both, see *Praise*, ch. XIII, 20 and my Introduction, above, xxvii.

[24] Aquinas, *On Princely Government* I.i (from Aristotle, *Politics*, I.i.9).

[25] Here again are the verbs 'providere' and 'intendere' which are an essential part of Fortescue's political vocabulary, taken from Aquinas, *On Princely Government*. See my Introduction, above, xxvii.

[26] This is Aristotle, *Physics* II.ii, but Fortescue probably got it either from *Auctoritates Aristotelis*, 142, or from pseudo-Aquinas, *De Regimine Principum* III.xi.

called, antonomastically, regal (*regiam*) dignity and power. Thus did the kingly highness (*culmen regium*) gets its origin and being, although under and from unbelievers, yet naturally and by the institution of the law of nature. And in as much as that which is always good and equitable is called right (*ius*) (*Of Justice and Right*)[27], the institution of the power of the king, by whomsoever it was made, was just (*iusta*), seeing it is held to be always not only good but equitable.

Holy scripture also suffers us not to doubt but that the Lord Himself ratified it, seeing that He delegated Angels for the protection of (*pro tutela*) the kingdoms which the nations formed as for the man whom He had created, as is evident from the ninth chapter of Daniel; and although it has been suspected by some that the princes of the Greeks and of the Persians who are there mentioned were bad Angels,[28] yet Vincent affirmed in his *On the Moral Education of the Prince* that St Gregory wrote that they were good Angels. Again, it was no small mark of approbation of heathen kingdoms, that God commanded Elijah the Prophet (III Kings ch.19) to anoint Hazael to be king of Syria, one of the Gentile kingdoms.[29]

A king ruling politically is of equal power and liberty with a king ruling royally[30]

And although a king ruling politically cannot change his laws (*leges*) without the assent of the chief men of his kingdom, yet when they are deficient he fills their place. But let not the Royal Law (*Lex Regia*) on that account exalt itself, thinking itself freer or more powerful than the Political Law (*Lege Politica*), or its king freer or more powerful than a king governing the people politically, seeing that the ability to sin does not belong to power, but is a dangerous impotence and slavery, as in the case of privation of sight or the ability to be ignorant of virtue. For if the breath of pride so affects the soul of man that, abandoning humility and modesty, he is raised into ambition and plundering of kingdoms, or if lust has so fired

---

[27] *CIC, Digest* I.I.I: 'ius est ars boni et aequi'.
[28] Daniel 9–11.
[29] I Kings 19:15.
[30] *On the Nature of the law of Nature* I.xxvi. The Latin is printed in Chrimes, *De laudibus*, 153–5 as well as in Clermont edn (1869).

his flesh that he lapses into luxury and lewdness, or if the crime of covetousness, or swelling of anger casts a man down into the villany of theft or murder, does not that man's sin then proceed from his impotence, seeing that unless he had surrendered himself as a conquest to those vices, such sins could not be accomplished? Thus also every sin with which a man is stained proceeds from the injustice of vice and the folly of man, by which he makes himself a slave to those vices; whence it must needs be confessed that it arises from the impotence of an idle and spiritless being. Wherefore to be able to sin is not power or liberty, no more than to be able to grow old or rotten, nor can he who is powerful to sin be called absolutely powerful, on account of the contrary quality contained in the adjunct, no more than a dead man can be called absolutely a man.

How conspicuous is then the sinner's impotence and how great is his slavery proved to be when he, first vanquished by evil vices affecting his mind, as though by tyrants too strong for him, through his own pusillanimity and sluggishness of soul, has yielded himself to them as a slave, as the Lord says – 'He who commits sin is the slave of sin.'[31] Whence afterwards by his own affections and passions (which the ancients call 'perturbations'), as though bound with chains, he is thrust down into the dungeon of slavery, concerning which Boethius writes thus in rhyme:

> For although the Indian land afar
> Trembles at your laws (*iura*),
> And furthest Thule serves you,
> Yet not to be able to banish black cares
> Or put to flight wretched lamentations,
> This is not power.[32]

And seeing that all the actions of man, as the aforesaid Boethius says in the fourth Book of *The Consolation of Philosophy*, are accomplished in two things, namely will and power (concerning which a rhymer says, 'Two things make all doings – will and power – put them asunder and they effect nothing'), it is evident that when a man has done a thing, he has had the will and power

---

[31] John 8:34.
[32] Boethius, *Consolation of Philosophy*, III.v. Thule was, to the Romans, the northern most limit of the known world and is sometimes also identified as Iceland or Mainland (Shetland Isles).

to do it, and if a man has wished to do a thing and not done it, he is judged of necessity to have been impotent in that thing. But in as much as the Supreme Goodness has so affected the nature of humankind in its beginning with His own goodness that man ever wishes for good (as the same Boethius says – 'Man, unless seduced by error, cannot wish for anything but what is good, which is distinguished as an object of the will'), it follows that, if a man forsakes the doing of good, it comes of impotence, since it cannot have proceeded from will.[33]

Wherefore, if it is good for every people to be governed by laws to which they themselves assent, it will be admitted of necessity that the rule of a king who governs his people by such laws, which is called a political government (*regimen politicum*), springs from the power, as it does also from the will of such a king. Wherefore, every such king is powerful, nor can he by reason of such a kind of government be called powerless or not free, seeing that what he wishes, he does, not hindered by any more powerful than himself.

Moreover, that it is good for a people to be regulated by such laws, St Thomas in the first book of his treatise above mentioned, seems to have most clearly taught. For when in that place he had condemned oligarchy, which is the rule of the few bad, and democracy, which is the rule of the many bad, and had preferred aristocracy, which is the rule of the few good, who are called *optimates*, to the rule of the many good, which is called *politia*, he adjudged monarchy, which is the rule of a single prince alone, to be the best rule of all. And as he held that rule to be the best of all under a good prince, so under a bad prince, which he himself calls a tyranny, he held it for the worst.[34] Wherefore finally, he seems in that place to wish that the government of a kingdom should be so disposed, that all occasion of tyranny should be withdrawn from the king, as well as that his power be so tempered that it decline not easily into tyranny,[35] by which words he is not only proved to say that it is good for a people to be ruled by laws to which it consents, but also himself to give no small commendation and approbation to the king ruling politically (*regis politice dominantis imperium*), in as much as

---

[33] This is all taken from Boethius, *Consolation of Philosophy*, IV.ii. Fortescue clearly knew more of this work than is contained in the *Auctoritates Aristotelis*.

[34] Aquinas, *On Princely Government*, I.iii.

[35] Aquinas, *On Princely Government*, I.vi.

such a king, proceeding according to the laws and customs of his kingdom, cannot easily be turned into a tyrant, and to rule a people in such a fashion can be no hindrance to the liberty of a king, even as it is no hindrance to the free will of the Angels, established in glory, that now they cannot desire to sin.

Wherefore it may be concluded without more delay that a king ruling politically, who is most firmly bound by the laws of his kingdom to just judgement, is a prince of no less power or liberty than a king ruling royally who, suffering no bridle, can freely be as wanton as he will. Since ability to sin is not power, and nor is political law, which is excellently well established with assent of the people, of less efficacy or virtue than royal law most equitably promulgated by the best of princes.

Appendix B
Example of how good council helps and advantages and of what follows from the contrary

This is an alternative version of chapter 16 of *The Governance*, above 117–18. It is taken from Yelverton MS 35 and was printed by Clermont (1869 edn) 475–6 and by Plummer (1885 edn), 347–8. I have modernised the spelling and punctuation of the original.

O what good wealth and prosperity should grow to the realm of England if such a council should be once perfectly established and the king guided thereby. The Romans who by wisdom and manhood got the lordship and monarchy of the world were first governed by kings; but when the kings through insolence, following their passions, left the council of the senate, the Romans rose upon them and put away their kings for evermore. And then they were ruled by the senators, and by consuls politically many years, by whose wisdom they got the lordship of a great part of the world. But after their great wealth, by division that fell between the consuls for lack of one head, they had amongst them civil battles, wherein at some one debate more than eighty thousand of them were slain and exiled. And after that they were governed by one head called an emperor, who, using in all his rule the council of the senate, got the monarchy of the world. So that at Christ's birth, the emperor commanded the whole world to be described as subjects unto him. Which lordship and monarchy the emperor kept all the while they were ruled by the council of the senate. But, after that, when the emperor left the council of the senate, and some of them, such as Nero, Domitian and others, had slain a great part of the senators, and were ruled by their private councillors, the estate of the emperor fell in decay, and their lordship has since grown less and less, so as now the emperor is not of as much might as is one of the kings which sometime were his subjects.

Wherefore also Englishmen, whose kings sometime were counselled by sober and well chosen councillors have been the mightiest kings of the world. But since our kings have been ruled by private councillors, such as have offered their service and counsel, and were not chosen thereto, we have not been able to keep our own livelihood, nor to vex those who have taken it from us. And that has been mostly for poverty and lack of goods. And we have had by that occasion civil wars amongst ourselves as had the Romans when they had not one head but many governors. And our realm is fallen thereby in decay and poverty, as was the Empire when the emperor left the council of the senate. But it may not be doubted that if our kings were to be counselled by such a wise established council as is before devised, and do thereafter as did the first emperor that got the monarchy of the world, we should first have unity and peace within our land, riches and prosperity, and be the mightiest and most wealthy realm of the world.

Appendix C
Articles to the Earl of Warwick 1470

The original is to be found in Yelverton MS 35. It is printed in Plummer, 1885 edn, 348–353. It repeats much of the material contained in *The Governance*.

Here follows in articles certain advertisements sent by my lord prince to the earl of Warwick his father-in-law, for to be shown and communicated by him to King Henry his father and his council, to the intent that the same advertisements, or such of them as may be thought expedient for the good public of the realm, can be practised and put in use.

1. First, forasmuch as many of the lords and other men in lower estate, which in this time of the king's great trouble have done him good service to their great charges and costs, and other of his faithful subjects, which for his sake and their true acquittal have suffered great harms in their persons and loss of their goods, will now sue to his highness both for rewards and for recompense of their harms, such as reason, liberality and above all royal munificence would they should have. Yet if the king by such consideration gives to some man and not to another, who for the same reason ought to be rewarded, there shall grow great grudge amongst his people. And also some man, with importunity of suit, and by partial means, shall be able to obtain greater rewards than they have deserved, and yet complain, seeing they have too little. And some men for lack of means toward his highness should have too little, or nothing at all. It is thought therefore good that all such rewards and recompenses

should be deferred until a council is established; and then the supplications of all such persons can be sent by the king to the said council, where every man's merit may be indifferently examined. And then the council may first consider, what livelihood the king has for the sustenance of his estate, and how distribution may be made from the remnant amongst such as have deserved weal, so that the king by reason of liberality and rewards does not diminish nor so lose his livelihood, that by necessity he is compelled to live upon his commons and upon the Church, to his infamy and the withdrawing from him of the hearts of his subjects, which God wills not. And then, when the king upon all such supplication is fully advertised by his council, he may so reward every man as he has deserved, and as the king's livelihood will extend to it. For if this order is kept, no man may grudge with the king's highness nor with the lords nor with any other man about his person as they were accustomed to do.[1]

2. It is thought good that it should please the king to establish a council of twelve spiritual men and twelve temporal men, of the most wise and indifferent that can be chosen in all the land. And that there should be chosen to them yearly four lords spiritual and four lords temporal, or in less number. And that the king should do no great thing touching the rule of his realm, nor give land, fee, office or benefice, but that first his intent therein shall be imparted to and disputed in that council, and that he shall have heard their advice thereupon; which may in no thing restrain his power, liberty or prerogative. And then shall the king not be counselled by men of his chamber, of his household, nor others who cannot counsel him; but the good public shall by wise men be conducted to the prosperity and honour of the land, to the security and welfare of the king, and to the security of all those who are about his person, whom the people have often slain for the miscounselling of their sovereign lord. But the aforesaid twenty-four councillors may take no fee, clothing, nor rewards, nor be in any man's service, otherwise than as the justices of the law may do. Many other articles need to be added hereto which are now too long to be remembered herein. Nevertheless it is thought that the great officers, such as chancellor, treasurer, and privy seal, the judges, barons of the exchequer, and

---

[1] Cf. *Governance*, ch.14, above 112–14.

the clerk of the rolls, may be of this council when they will come thereto, or when the said twenty-four and eight lords will desire them to be with them.[2]

3. And forasmuch as it may be thought that the establishment of such a council shall be a new and a great charge to the king, it is to be considered, that the old council in England, which was mostly of great lords who attended more to their own matters than to the good universal profit, and therefore procured themselves to be of the council which was almost of as great charge to the king as this council shall be and nothing of such profit. For this council shall almost continually study and labour upon the good politic weal of the land, so as to provide that the money be not borne out of the realm, and how bullion may be brought in, how merchandise and commodities of the land may keep their prices and value, how foreigners cast not down the price of the commodities growing in the land, and other such points of policy. And also how the law may be formally kept and reformed there as it is defective, to the greatest good and security of the wealth of the land that has been seen in any land. And truly there has been given recently to some one lord temporal much more livelihood in yearly value than will pay the wages of all the new council. And also the spiritual men of this new council shall not need to have as great wages as the temporal men, which when they come to the council must leave in their countries one household for their wives, children, and servants, or else carry them with them, which the spiritual men need not to do. By which consideration the spiritual men in the court of parliament of Paris have but three hundred scutes, whereas the temporal men have four hundred.[3]

4. It is necessary that before any grants are made by the king from any part of his livelihood, there should first be assigned particularly certain livelihood for the king's house, for his chapel, and for his wardrobe. And other livelihood for the payment of his courts, his council, and all other ordinary charges; so that no part thereof is restrained to any other use, until all the charges are yearly paid. And if any patent is made to any other use of any part of that livelihood, that patent should be void and of no effect. And also

---

[2] Cf. *Governance*, ch.15, above 114–17.
[3] Cf. *Governance*, ch.15, above 114–17.

that no patent should be made in inheritance of any part of the king's livelihood, by what title so ever that it comes to him, without the assent of his parliament, nor for term of life, or years countervailing term of life, without the advice of his council, except such patents as shall be made of farms by the treasurer of England, bailiffs and other officers having power to approve the king's livelihood. And the chancellor who shall fortune to enseal any patent contrary hereto, shall lose his office and forfeit to the king all his livelihood temporal. And that the same patent shall be void. And moreover that every chancellor shall have like punishment if he enseals any patent for any other matter, or that matter is debated in the king's council, and he certified of the manner and conclusion of their deliberation upon the same. And if the same matter have been thought to the council good, the chancellor may write in the patent which he shall make thereof that it is passed by the advice and assent of the council, and else he shall leave these words, and write in the patent only that the matter has been debated in the king's council.[4]

5. Likewise when there is livelihood sufficient for the payment of the king's house, the expenses thereof may be always paid in hand, which expenses shall be from thenceforward of so reasonable a price that the fourth part of the old expenses of the same household should be yearly saved. And the king shall have thereby always the market at his gate to his great profit, but to much more profit of the poor people. And to the singular pleasure of God, who has no prince excused of paying of his debts, and especially for his victuals.[5]

6. Likewise it is thought good that the king gives not one of his offices, though it be but a parkership, to any man save only to his own servants, and that every of his officers shall be sworn that he is with no man in service, nor has nor will take of any man while he serves the king, pension, fee, or clothing, except only of the king. For then the king shall have wholly the might of his land, which is most ruled by his officers as they have been before these days. And the king shall then be able to reward with offices, those who ought to be rewarded, without diminishing of his revenues of

---

[4] Cf. *Governance*, ch.6, above 94–7.
[5] Cf. *Governance*, ch.5, above 92–3.

his crown. And it shall be good that no man shall have two offices, except the servants and officers of the king's house, which may have, when they deserve it, a parkership or such another office as they may well keep by a sufficient deputy. Which deputy shall then be sworn to serve no other man save his master who serves the king. And in like form the king may reward his temporal councillors with such offices when he will. For it is not likely but that he will advance the spiritual men of his council with benefices, as they shall be worthy.[6]

7. Likewise forasmuch as the king is now in great poverty, and may not presently sustain the expenses of so great a household as he sometimes kept, nor is he presently purveyed of vessels and other household goods honourable and convenient for him; and also his costs now upon the establishments of his realm will be greater than any man can estimate with certainty; it is thought good that it will please his highness to forbear all his first year the keeping of his worshipful and great household; and be in all that time in such a sure place or places as his most noble grace can think best for his health and pleasure, with few people, and without recalling and taking again in all that year of the servants of his old household, but such as necessity shall cause him. For if he take within that time any of them, the remnant will grudge for their absence. And also those that are thus taken will not leave importune suit to have unto them all their old fellowship, which shall be troublesome and a great annoyance to himself, and to all those that shall be about him for that year.

---

[6] Cf. *Governance*, ch.17, above 118–21.

Index

Index

Index

Index

Index

Cambridge Texts in the History of Political Thought

Titles published in the series thus far

Aristotle *The Politics* and *The Constitution of Athens* (edited by Stephen Everson)

Arnold *Culture and Anarchy and other Writings* (edited by Stefan Collini)

Astell *Political Writings* (edited by Patricia Springborg)

Austin *The Province of Jurisprudence Determined* (edited by Wilfrid E. Rumble)

Bakunin *Statism and Anarchy* (edited by Marshall Shatz)

Baxter *A Holy Commonwealth* (edited by William Lamont)

Beccaria *On Crimes and Punishments and other Writings* (edited by Richard Bellamy)

Bentham *A Fragment on Government* (introduction by Ross Harrison)

Bernstein *The Preconditions of Socialism* (edited by Henry Tudor)

Bodin *On Sovereignty* (edited by Julian H. Franklin)

Bossuet *Politics Drawn from the Very Words of Holy Scripture* (edited by Patrick Riley)

Burke *Pre-Revolutionary Writings* (edited by Ian Harris)

Christine de Pizan *The Book of the Body Politic* (edited by Kate Langdon Forhan)

Cicero *On Duties* (edited by M. T. Griffin and E. M. Atkins)

Constant *Political Writings* (edited by Biancamaria Fontana)

Dante *Monarchy* (edited by Prue Shaw)

Diderot *Political Writings* (edited by John Hope Mason and Robert Wokler)

The Dutch Revolt (edited by Martin van Gelderen)

The Early Political Writings of the German Romantic (edited by Frederick C. Beiser)

Early Greek Political Thought from Homer to the Sophists (edited by Michael Gagarin and Paul Woodruff)

Ferguson *An Essay on the History of Civil Society* (edited by Fania Oz-Salzberger)

Filmer *Patriarcha and other Writings* (edited by Johann P. Sommerville)

Sir John Fortescue *On the Laws and Governance of England* (edited by Shelley Lockwood)

Fourier *The Theory of the Four Movements* (edited by Gareth Stedman Jones and Ian Patterson)

Gramsci *Pre-Prison Writings* (edited by Richard Bellamy)

Guicciardini *Dialogue on the Government of Florence* (edited by Alison Brown)

Harrington *A Commonwealth of Oceana* and *A System of Politics* (edited by J. G. A. Pocock)

Hegel *Elements of the Philosophy of Right* (edited by Allen W. Wood and H. B. Nisbet)

Hobbes *Leviathan* (edited by Richard Tuck)

Hobhouse *Liberalism and other Writings* (edited by James Meadowcroft)

Hooker *Of the Laws of Ecclesiastical Polity* (edited by A. S. McGrade)

Hume *Political Essays* (edited by Knud Haakonssen)

King James VI and I *Political Writings* (edited by Johann P. Sommerville)

John of Salisbury *Policraticus* (edited by Cary Nederman)

Kant *Political Writings* (edited by H. S. Reiss and H. B. Nisbet)

Knox *On Rebellion* (edited by Roger A. Mason)

Kropotkin *The Conquest of Bread and other Writings* (edited by Marshall Shatz)

Lawson *Politica sacra et civilis* (edited by Conal Condren)

Leibniz *Political Writings* (edited by Patrick Riley)

Locke *Two Treatises of Government* (edited by Peter Laslett)

Loyseau *A Treatise of Orders and Plain Dignities* (edited by Howell A. Lloyd)

Luther and Calvin on Secular Authority (edited by Harro Höpfl)

Machiavelli *The Prince* (edited by Quentin Skinner and Russell Price)

de Maistre *Considerations on France* (edited by Isaiah Berlin and Richard Lebrun)

Malthus *An Essay on the Principle of Population* (edited by Donald Winch)

Marsiglio of Padua *Defensor minor* and *De translatione Imperii* (edited by Cary Nederman)

Marx *Early Political Writings* (edited by Joseph O'Malley)

Marx *Later Political Writings* (edited by Terence Carver)

James Mill *Political Writings* (edited by Terence Ball)

J. S. Mill *On Liberty*, with *The Subjection of Women* and *Chapters on Socialism* (edited by Stefan Collini)

Milton *Political Writings* (edited by Martin Dzelzainis)

Montesquieu *The Spirit of the Laws* (edited by Anne M. Cohler, Basia Carolyn Miller and Harold Samuel Stone)

More *Utopia* (edited by George M. Logan and Robert M. Adams)

Morris *News from Nowhere* (edited by Krishan Kumar)

Nicholas of Cusa *The Catholic Concordance* (edited by Paul E. Sigmund)

Nietzsche *On the Genealogy of Morality* (edited by Keith Ansell-Pearson)

Paine *Political Writings* (edited by Bruce Kuklick)

Plato *Statesman* (edited by Julia Annas and Robin Waterfield)

Price *Political Writings* (edited by D. O. Thomas)

Priestley *Political Writings* (edited by Peter Miller)

Proudhon *What is Property?* (edited by Donald R. Kelley and Bonnie G. Smith)

Pufendorf *On the Duty of Man and Citizen According to Natural Law* (edited by James Tully)

The Radical Reformation (edited by Michael G. Baylor)

Seneca *Moral and Political Essays* (edited by John Cooper and John Procope)

Sidney *Court Maxims* (edited by Hans W. Blom, Eco Haitsma Mulier and Ronald Janse)

Spencer *Man versus the State* and *The Proper Sphere of Government* (edited by John Offer)

Stirner *The Ego and its Own* (edited by David Leopold)

Thoreau *Political Writings* (edited by Nancy Rosenblum)

Utopias of the British Enlightenment (edited by Gregory Claeys)

Vitoria *Political Writings* (edited by Anthony Pagden and Jeremy Lawrance)

Voltaire *Political Writings* (edited by David Williams)

Weber *Political Writings* (edited by Peter Lassman and Ronald Speirs)

William of Ockham *A Short Discourse on Tyrannical Government* (edited by A. S. McGrade and John Kilcullen)

William of Ockham *A Letter to the Friars Minor and other Writings* (edited by A. S. McGrade and John Kilcullen)

Wollstonecraft *A Vindication of the Rights of Men* and *A Vindication of the Rights of Woman* (edited by Sylvana Tomaselli)